PostgreSQL Basic Training
for
Application Developers

Robert Wingate

ISBN 13: 9781706557258

Disclaimer

The content of this book is based upon the author's understanding of and experience with the PostgreSQL product. Every attempt has been made to provide correct information. However, the author and publisher do not guarantee the accuracy of every detail, nor do they assume responsibility for information included in or omitted from it. All of the information in this book should be used at your own risk.

Copyright

The contents of this book may not be copied in whole, or in part, without the explicit written permission of the author. The contents are intended for personal use only. Secondary distribution for gain is not allowed. Any alteration of the contents is absolutely forbidden.

ISBN: 9781706557258

Contents

Introduction

Welcome
Congratulations on your purchase of PostgreSQL Basic Training for Application Developers. This book will help you learn the essential information you need to know about PostgreSQL so you can be productive as soon as possible. You'll receive instruction, examples and exercises to help you learn and to gauge your readiness for development work on a PostgreSQL technical team.

Assumptions:
While I do not assume that you know a great deal about PostgreSQL, I do assume that you've worked in a Linux, UNIX or Windows environment and know your way around. We'll be using the Windows environment in this book.

Also I assume that you have a working knowledge of the JAVA programming language which we will use for all the programming examples (in most cases I also created parallel c# .NET examples). All in all, I assume you have:

1. A working knowledge of Windows (or Unix/Linux) files and navigation
2. A basic understanding of SQL
3. Proficiency using either Java or c# .NET
4. Access to a computer running Windows 7 or higher (or UNIX/LINUX)

Knowledge of PostgreSQL
If you are a beginner, this book should give you what you need to get started, and to develop a solid PostgreSQL developer foundation. Even if you have years of experience with PostgreSQL, you may find new techniques and ways of accomplishing things in PostgreSQL.

Experience with PostgreSQL
I include instructions for downloading and installing the components required to run PostgreSQL on your local Windows computer. That way you can follow along with the examples given in this text. You can also come up with your own training project and work through it at your own pace.

Knowledge and experience. Will that guarantee that you'll succeed as a PostgreSQL application developer? Of course, nothing is guaranteed in life. But if you put sufficient effort into a well-rounded study plan that includes both of the above, I believe you have a very good chance of excelling as an application developer in the PostgreSQL world.

Best of luck!

Robert Wingate

IBM Certified Application Developer – DB2 11 for z/OS

Chapter One: PostgreSQL Installation and Tools

Welcome to PostgreSQL Basic Training for Application Developers! Before we get into development activities, I want to introduce you to the environment we'll be working in. If you've ever used PostgreSQL, you've almost certainly encountered these tools. But let's make sure we're all familiar with how to install and access PostgreSQL, and how to use the basic PostgreSQL tools available.

The PostgreSQL database and pgAdmin tool are available for free. You can download a bundle that includes both here:

https://www.enterprisedb.com/downloads/postgres-postgresql-downloads

When this window comes up, select the appropriate column based upon your machine and click on the Download link for version 12.

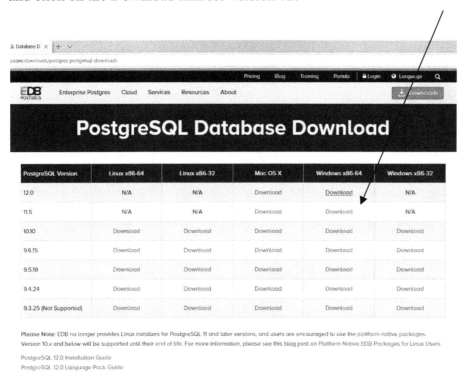

When the download is finished, locate the file in your downloads folder. Right click on the file and run it (I suggest you run as Administrator).

PostgreSQLInstall

Name	Date modified	Type	Size
postgresql-12.0-1-windows-x64.exe	10/28/2019 8:47 PM	Application	190,875 KB

You'll see this screen. Click **Next**.

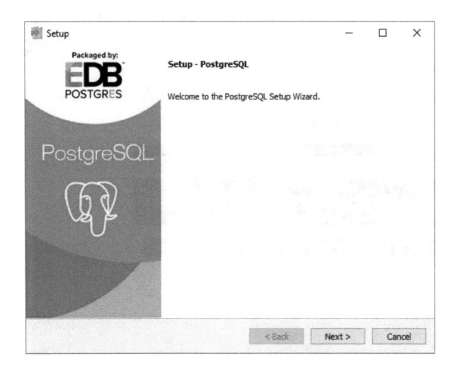

Specify an installation directory or accept the default. Click **Next.**

Choose the components you wish to install. I recommend choosing all of them.
Click **Next**.

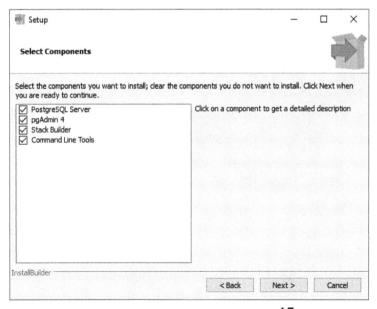

Specify a password for the database superuser **postgres**. In my case I used **posrgres** as the password. I do not recommend doing this in a shared environment. But for training purposes we can keep things simple. Click **Next**.

I recommend that you accept the default port. Click **Next**.

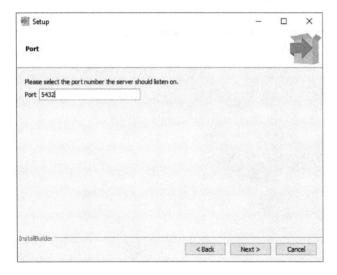

I recommend that you accept the default database cluster. Click **Next**.

Review your pre-installation summary, then click **Next**.

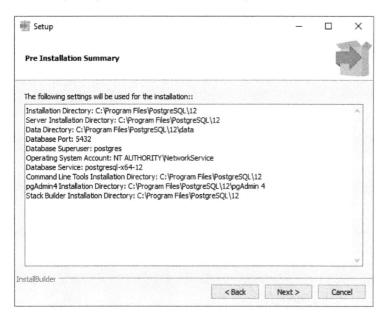

Click **Next**.

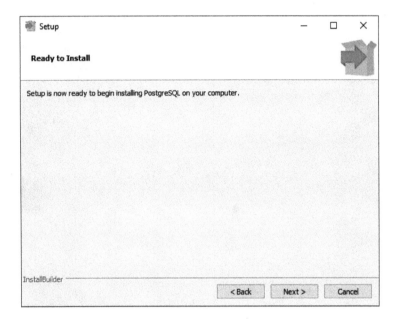

The installations will begin.

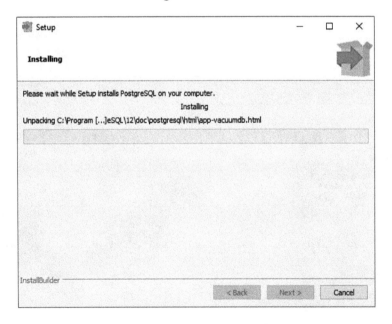

Monitor the installation. It will take several minutes.

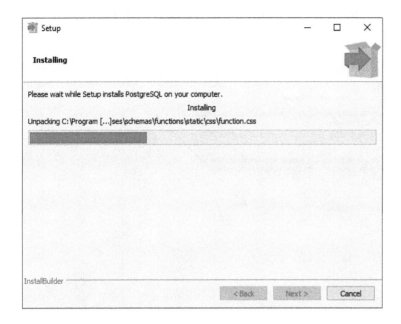

Click **Finish**.

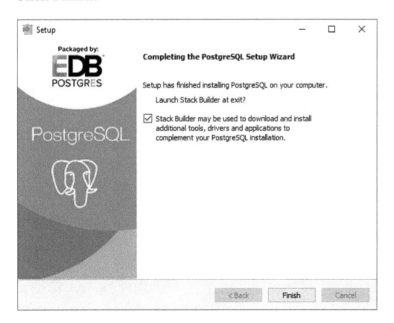

You'll now be prompted as to whether you want to install other supplementary products. I that recommend you do so. First, use the pull down menu to select your installed version of PostgreSQL.

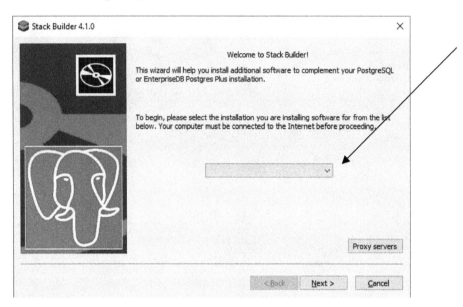

Once you've selected the installation, click **Next**.

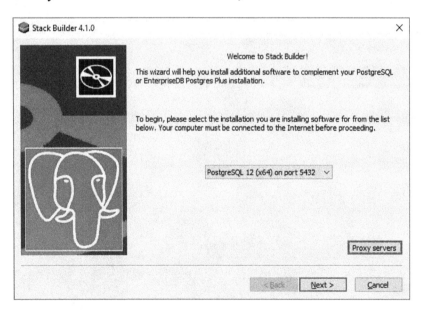

Select those add on products that you wish to install. I recommend installing at least the JDBC and ODBC drivers. Click **Next**.

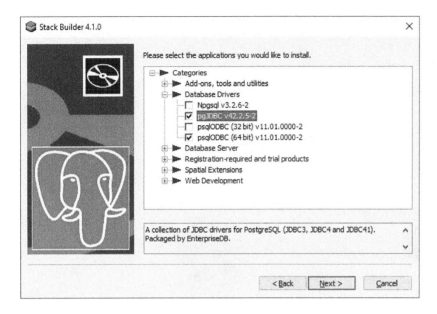

Click **Next.**

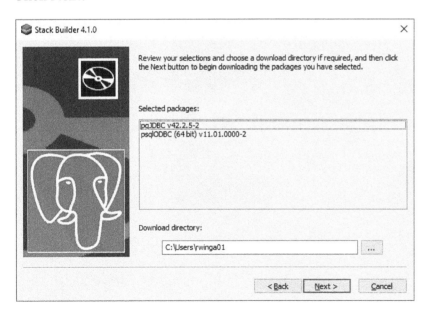

The products will be downloaded.

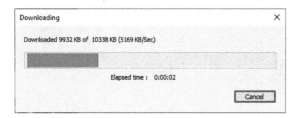

Click **Next.**

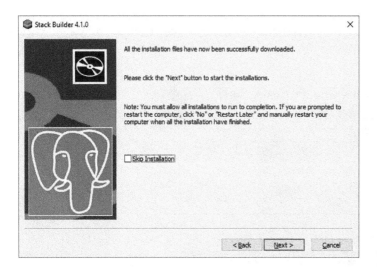

Click **Next** to install the JDBC driver.

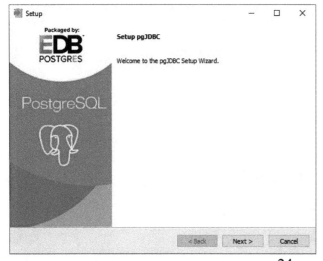

Accept the default installation directory or type in a different directory. Click **Next.**

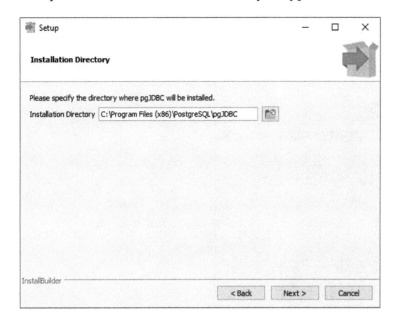

Click **Next.**

The JDBC product will be installed.

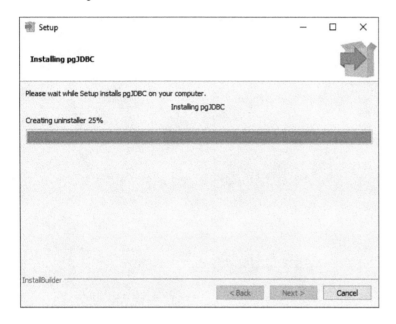

Click **Finish**.

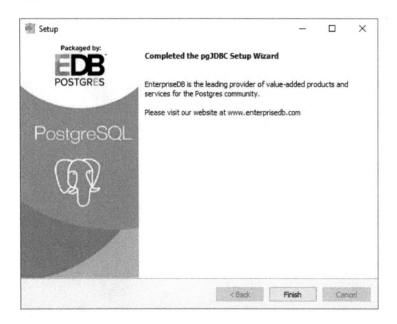

Pause for a bit. The ODBC installation window should open. It may take a few minutes. When you see this window, click **Next**.

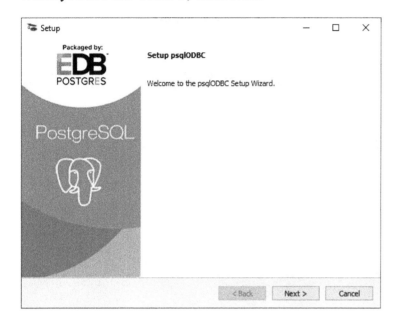

Enter an installation directory or accept the default. Click **Next**.

Click **Next**.

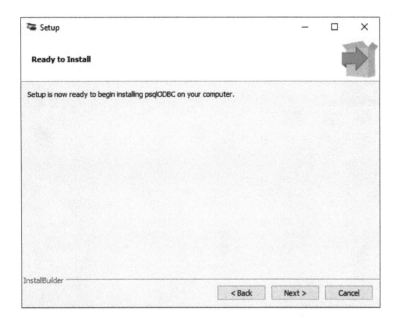

Click **Finish**.

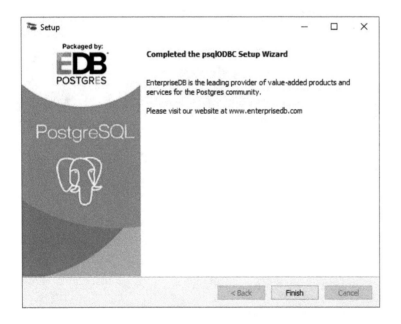

Switch to the Stack Builder window. Click **Finish**.

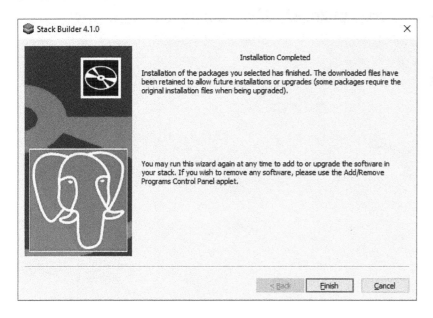

I'll repeat this later in the textbook, but your JDBC jar file will be placed in the installation directory that you specified. The file name you'll be looking for is postgresql-<version mame>.jar.

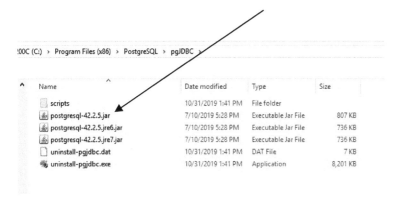

We are not quite done yet. We still need to install the .NET drivers for PostgreSQL. To do this, from the start menu, select **PostgreSQL 12 → Application Stack Builder**.

Use the Database Drivers pull down, and select the **Npgsql** product. Then click **Next**.

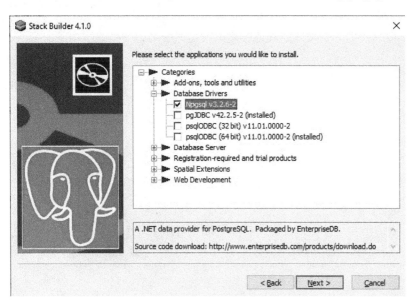

Click **Next**.

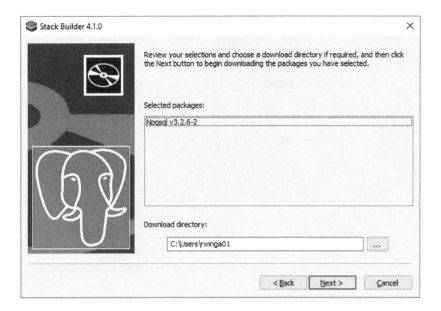

Click **Next**.

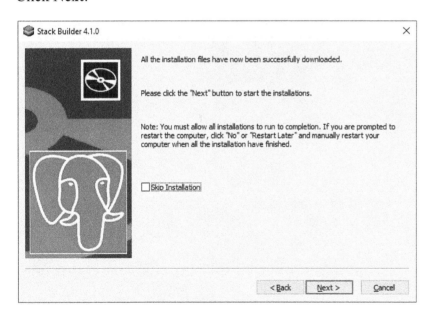

Click **Next**.

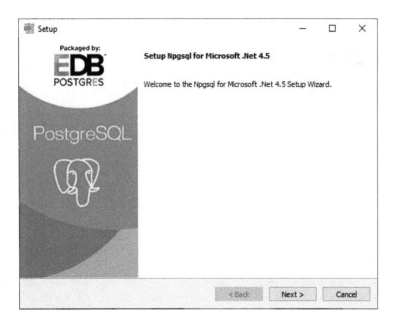

Select an installation directory, or accept the default. Click **Next**.

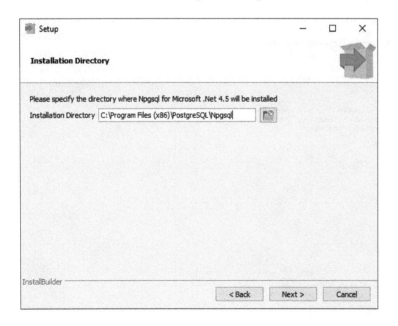

Click **Next.**

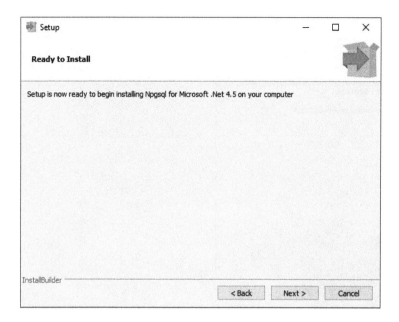

Monitor the installation.

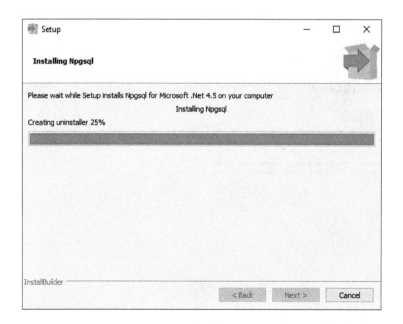

Click Finish.

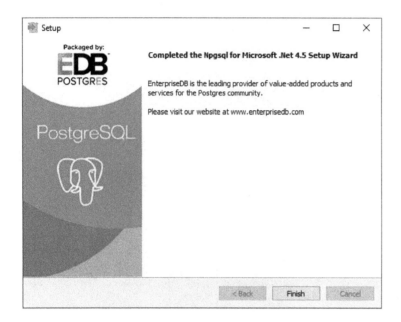

Go back to the Stack Builder dialog and click **Finish**.

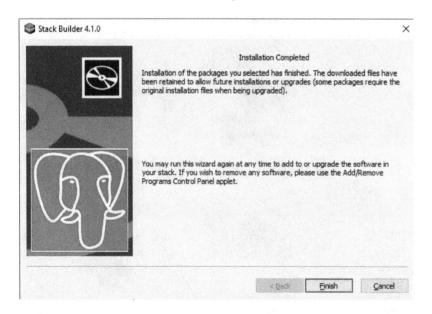

We'll go over the location of the .NET driver DLL when we get to programming in chapter four.

Now we are ready to open PgAdmin.

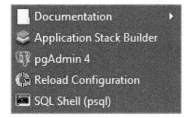

You'll be prompted to enter the master password. I set mine as **postgres** on installation.

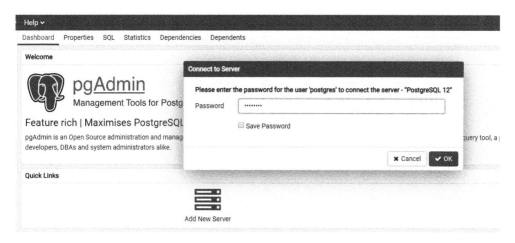

Now you're in the main pgAdmin window. Click on **Databases** in the object tree to expand it.

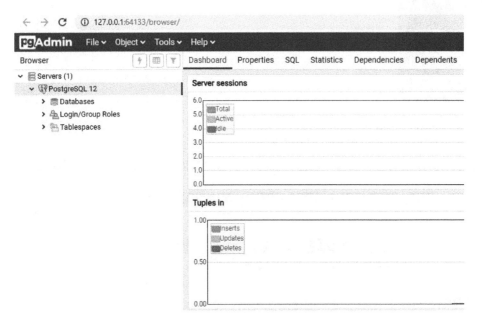

Currently there is only one database which is the **postgres** database. Let's create a new one called **DBHR** (database for human resources).

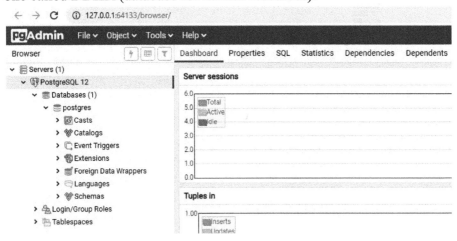

Right click on databases, and then select **Create → Database.**

Enter **DBHR** as the database name. Also add the description as below. Then click **Save.**

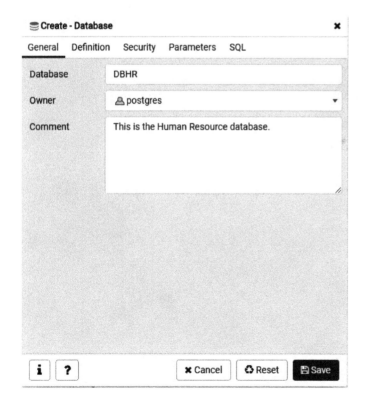

Congratulations, you've just created your first PostgreSQL database! If you refresh the list of databases, you'll see it.

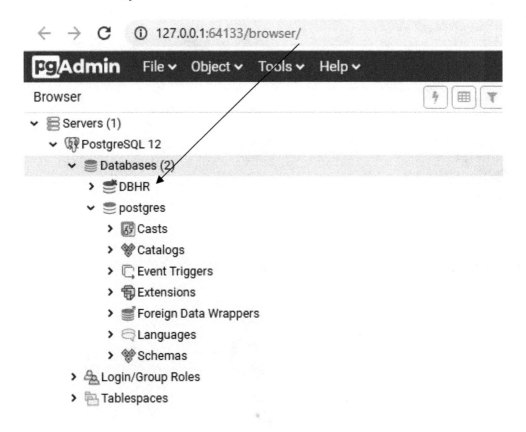

Click on the DBHR database to connect to it. You'll see the categories for the various object types in the tree.

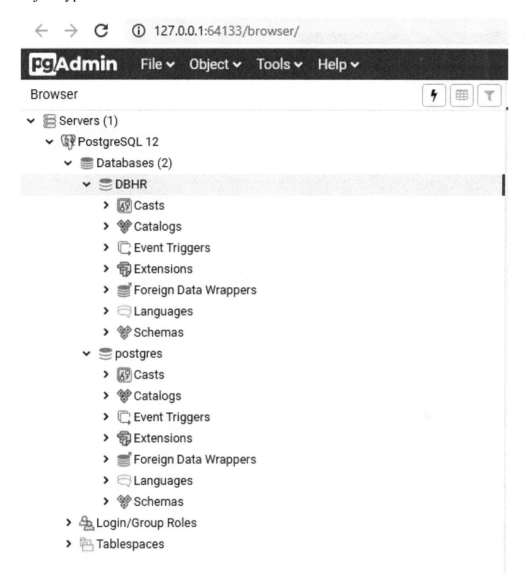

If you'd like you can create a script that could be used to create this same database, right click on the DBHR database and then select **CREATE Script**.

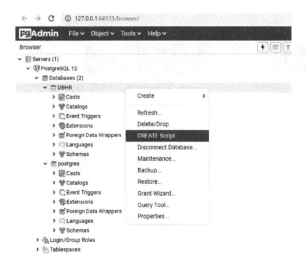

You'll see the precise DDL that was generated to create this database. If you drop the database you can recreate it any time by simply executing this script.

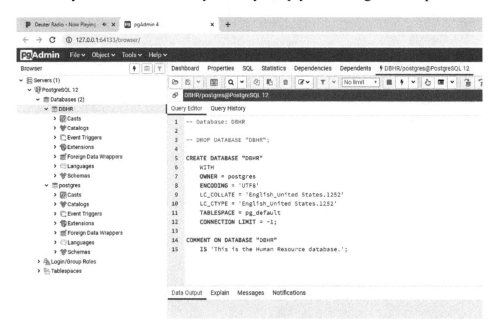

Our installation of the database and IDE is complete. If you like you can keep the PgAdmin open. We'll use it in the next chapter.

Chapter Two: Data Definition Language

Before rushing into programming it is a good idea to understand data types, and how to create and maintain the basic PostgreSQL objects. Often your DBA will handle this but it's best for application developers to understand the basic properties of the various objects (tables, indexes, views).

Database

A PostgreSQL database is a collection of objects including, tables, indexes, views, triggers and stored procedures. Generally a database is concerned with a single domain such as marketing, accounting, shipping and receiving, etc. For purposes of this text book, we will be supporting a simple computerized human resource system that tracks employee information for a fictitious company.

CREATE

You can create a database with the CREATE DATABASE statement. The required syntax to create the database we created earlier (DBHR) is:

```
CREATE DATABASE <database name>
WITH
OWNER = <userid which will own the database>
ENCODING = <encoding scheme - default is 'UTF8'>
LC_COLLATE = <local collation value - default is 'English_United States.1252'>
LC_CTYPE = <local collation type - default is 'English_United States.1252'>
TABLESPACE = <tablespace name - default is pg_default>
CONNECTION LIMIT = <connection limits, if any, where -1 is no limits>;
```

You model your database on another existing database. FALLBACK means that duplicate copies of data rows in the table are saved for backup purposes. ACCOUNT is associated with a userid which in this case will be DBHR.

```
CREATE DATABASE "DBHR"
WITH
OWNER = postgres
ENCODING = 'UTF8'
LC_COLLATE = 'English_United States.1252'
LC_CTYPE = 'English_United States.1252'
TABLESPACE = pg_default
CONNECTION LIMIT = -1;
```

If you did not create the DBHR database in the last chapter, please go ahead and do that now. If you did create it, but closed the PgAdmin, let's now reopen open PgAdmin. Select the DBHR database.

ALTER

If you need to change something on your database you use the ALTER statement. For example, to set the connection limit to 10 on our DBHR database we could issue this command:

```
ALTER DATABASE "DBHR" WITH CONNECTION LIMIT 10;
```

DROP

Most database objects can be removed/deleted by issuing the DROP command. The syntax to delete a database is very simple:

```
DROP DATABASE <databasename>
```

You could DROP the DBHR database by simply issuing this command:

```
DROP DATABASE DBHR;
```

We won't drop the DBHR database yet because we are going to use it throughout this chapter.

Schema

Your DBA will create an assign a schema for you – all your objects such as tables, indexes and views will be prefixed with the schema. PUBLIC is the default schema in PostgreSQL. If you do not specify a schema, all your objects will be created under PUBLIC. We will take this approach for basic training.

Tables

As I'm sure you are aware, a table is the basic structure and container for PostgreSQL data. Let's summarize the four different types of tables in PostgreSQL.

Permanent

A table structure which physically stores records.

Global Temporary

A table that is created and exists only for the duration of a user session. The definition of the table is retained in the data dictionary.

We'll look at an example of each of these.

DDL for Tables

CREATE

The basic syntax to create a PostgreSQL table specifies the table name and column specifications.

```
CREATE TABLE <tablename> (table specifications)
```

Create Permanent Table

For an example, let's create the first permanent table for our HR application. Here are the columns and data types for our table which we will name EMPLOYEE. We'll establish that the primary key is EMP_ID and that they key must be unique.

Field Name	Type	Attributes
EMP_ID	INTEGER	NOT NULL, PRIMARY KEY, UNIQUE
EMP_LAST_NAME	VARCHAR(30)	NOT NULL
EMP_FIRST_NAME	VARCHAR(20)	NOT NULL
EMP_SERVICE_YEARS	INTEGER	NOT NULL, DEFAULT IS ZERO
EMP_PROMOTION_DATE	DATE	

We can create this table using pgAdmin by right clicking on tables under the PUBLIC schema, and selecting the **Create → Table** option.

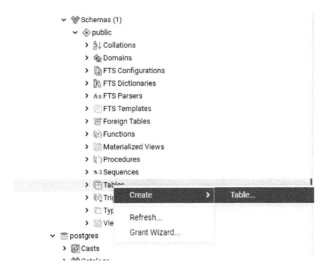

You'll see this dialog.

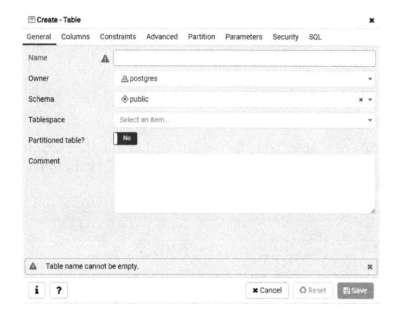

Now enter EMPLOYEE for the table name, select the pg_default tablespace and enter a description for the table. Then click on the Columns section near the top.

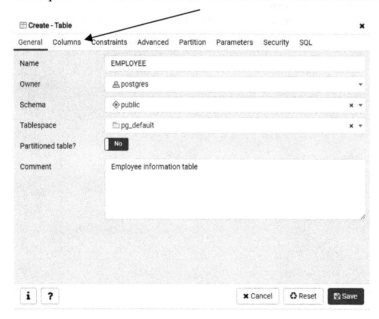

You can add columns to the table by clicking the + icon in the upper right hand side of the screen.

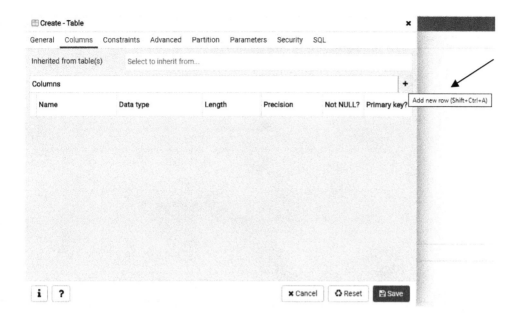

Now enter the first column which is EMP_ID. You must select a data type using the drop down selection box. EMP_ID will be an integer.

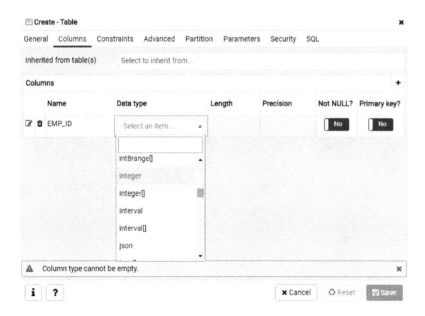

Also this will be the primary key for the table, so click on the Primary Key toggle switch to make it so.

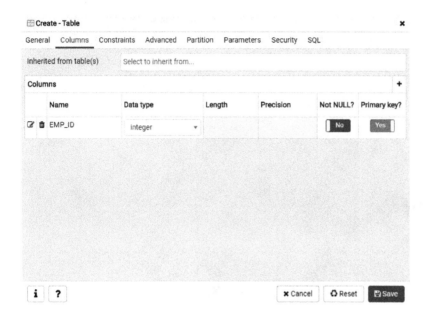

Go ahead and enter the other columns. When you've finished, your dialog should look like this. Click on **Save.**

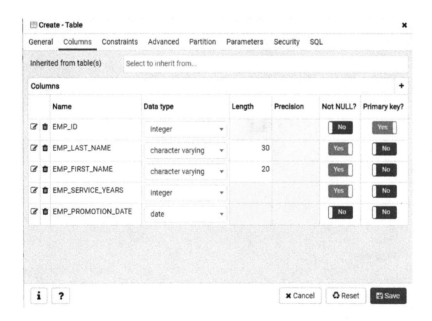

Your table is created. If you want to see the DDL that was generated to create the table, right click on the table name in the tree, and then select **SCRIPTS → CREATE**.

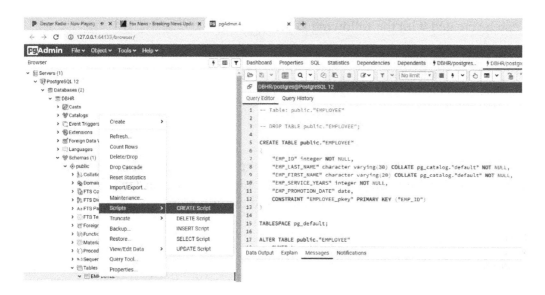

You'll see the DDL in the Query Editor. You could copy and save this script should you ever need to run it again.

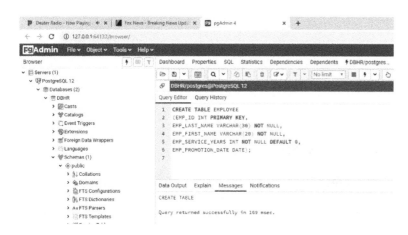

Now let's delete this table by right clicking on the table name in the tree, and selecting **Delete/Drop.** Next, we'll create the same table by executing a simplified version of the DDL and taking default values.

Now let's look at the basic DDL that is used to manage tables. As with other PostgreSQL objects, we use the CREATE, ALTER and DROP statements to create, change and delete tables respectively.

The table can be created with the following DDL:

```
CREATE TABLE EMPLOYEE
(EMP_ID INT PRIMARY KEY,
EMP_LAST_NAME VARCHAR(30) NOT NULL,
EMP_FIRST_NAME VARCHAR(20) NOT NULL,
EMP_SERVICE_YEARS INT NOT NULL DEFAULT 0,
EMP_PROMOTION_DATE DATE);
```

For the rest of the chapter, I will simply provide the DDL instead ofscreen shots. To create these objects you are welcome to use the pgAdmin wizards or simply execute the DDL. With that said, let's add a couple of records to the table.

```
INSERT INTO EMPLOYEE
VALUES (3217,
'JOHNSON',
'EDWARD',
4,
'2017-01-01');
```

```
INSERT INTO EMPLOYEE
VALUES (7459,
'STEWART',
'BETTY',
7,
'2016-07-31');
```

Let's verify that the records were added:

```
SELECT * FROM EMPLOYEE ORDER BY EMP_ID;
```

EMP_ID	EMP_LAST_NAME	EMP_FIRST_NAME	EMP_SERVICE_YEARS	EMP_PROMOTION_DATE
3217	JOHNSON	EDWARD	4	2017-01-01
7459	STEWART	BETTY	7	2016-07-31

Before we move on, let's create a couple more tables that we will use later. Let's say we need an EMP_PAY table to store the employee's annual pay, and an EMP_PAY_CHECK table that will be used to create pay checks on the first and fifteen of the month. Here's the DDL for these:

```
CREATE TABLE EMP_PAY(
EMP_ID INT NOT NULL,
EMP_REGULAR_PAY DECIMAL (8,2) NOT NULL,
EMP_BONUS_PAY DECIMAL (8,2));
```

```
CREATE TABLE EMP_PAY_CHECK(
EMP_ID INT NOT NULL,
EMP_REGULAR_PAY DECIMAL (8,2) NOT NULL,
EMP_SEMIMTH_PAY DECIMAL (8,2) NOT NULL);
```

Create Temporary Table

Now let's create a global temporary table. Here's a sample:

```
CREATE GLOBAL TEMPORARY TABLE EMP_PAY_DATA
(EMP_ID INT,
EMP_ANN_SALARY DECIMAL (8,2) NOT NULL)
ON COMMIT PRESERVE ROWS;

INSERT INTO EMP_PAY_DATA
VALUES (3217, 85000.00);
INSERT INTO EMP_PAY_DATA
VALUES (7459, 80000.00);
INSERT INTO EMP_PAY_DATA
VALUES (9134, 70000.00);

SELECT * FROM EMP_PAY_DATA;
```

EMP_ID	EMP_ANN_SALARY
9134	70000
7459	80000
3217	85000

ALTER

You can change various aspects of a table using the ALTER command. ALTER is often used to add an index or additional columns, or top drop a column from a table. Here we add and then drop an XML column called EMP_PROFILE from our EMPLOYEE table.

```
ALTER TABLE EMPLOYEE
ADD EMP_PROFILE XML;
```

You could also remove a column by specifying DROP.

```
ALTER TABLE EMPLOYEE
DROP EMP_PROFILE;
```

DROP

You can remove a table completely by issuing the DROP command.

```
DROP TABLE <table name>
```

Indexes

Indexes are structures that provide a means of quickly locating a record in a table. One of the main reasons for having indexes is that they improve performance when accessing data randomly. There are other reasons as well which we'll explore now.

Benefits of Indexes

Indexes are beneficial in these ways:

1. Indexes improve performance in that it is typically faster to use the index row locator to navigate to a specific row than to do a table scan (except in cases of very small tables).

2. Unique indexes ensure uniqueness of record keys (either primary or secondary).

Types of Indexes

The types of indexes available in PostgreSQL are as follows.

B-tree: the default index, applicable for types that can be sorted
Hash: handles equality only
GiST: suitable for non-scalar data types (e.g. geometrical shapes, fts, arrays)
SP-GiST: space partitioned GIST, an evolution of GiST for handling non-balanced structures (quadtrees, k-d trees, radix trees)
GIN: suitable for complex types (e.g. jsonb, fts, arrays)
BRIN: a relatively new type of index which supports data that can be sorted by storing min/max values in each block

For our basic training we will only be using the B-tree type indices, which are the most common. Note also that an index may be created to enforce uniqueness or not. A unique index enforces the rule that every row must contain a unique value in the indexed column. A non-unique index allows duplicate values to exist for the indexed column. A likely candidate for a unique index would be an employee number or social security number. A good example of a non-unique index could be postal zip code.

Examples of Indexes

Primary Key
Most tables include a unique primary index. For the example of our EMPLOYEE table earlier in the chapter, we defined the EMP_ID as the primary key. However, even if the column we want to use is not the primary key, we can establish a unique index on it, as we shall

see in the secondary index coming up next.

```
CREATE TABLE EMPLOYEE(
EMP_ID INT PRIMARY KEY,
EMP_LAST_NAME VARCHAR(30) NOT NULL,
EMP_FIRST_NAME VARCHAR(20) NOT NULL,
EMP_SERVICE_YEARS INT NOT NULL DEFAULT 0,
EMP_PROMOTION_DATE DATE);
```

Secondary Index

A secondary index is any index that is not a primary key. For example we have an employee table for which the primary key is EMP_ID. However we might also need to have a social security number column for which we want to have a unique index. The index on social security number will be a secondary index.

We could accomplish this by adding column EMP_SSN to the table, and then creating a unique index on it. Here's the DDL to do this:

```
ALTER TABLE EMPLOYEE
ADD EMP_SSN CHAR(09);
```

If any records exist in the table, we must first assign unique EMP_SSN values to the records in the table or our attempt to create a unique secondary index will fail.

```
UPDATE EMPLOYEE
SET EMP_SSN = '123456789'
WHERE EMP_ID = 3217;

UPDATE EMPLOYEE
SET EMP_SSN = '987654321'
WHERE EMP_ID = 7459;
```

Now let's create the unique secondary index on EMP_SSN. You can provide a name for the index or let PostgreSQL provide the name.

```
CREATE UNIQUE INDEX IDX_EMP_SSN ON EMPLOYEE (EMP_SSN);
```

Non-Unique Index

To create a non-unique index, you simply leave off the UNIQUE clause when specifying the secondary index for the table the table.

Data Types

PostgreSQL supports the following data types. You should be familiar with all of these so that you can choose the best data type for your purpose.

BOOLEAN

The BOOLEAN type can have one of three values: TRUE, FALSE and NULL. For examples you could create a column that indicates whether an employee is a current employee, and the values would be TRUE or FALSE.

Character Data Types

CHAR(n)

The character or CHAR data type stores fixed length character strings. You would use this for character data which is always the same length, such as state codes which are two bytes. The maximum length of a CHAR type is 64,000 bytes.

VARCHAR(n)

The VARCHAR type stores varying length character strings for which the maximum length is specified. For example VARCHAR(40) means between 1 and 40 bytes in length. A VARCHAR can be defined with a maximum of 64,000 bytes. If you need more, see the CLOB data type below under LOB data types.

TEXT

The TEXT data type can be used to store text that uses a single character set. This could include reports that need to be archived or any other text that exceeds the 64K limit imposed by the VARCHAR type. The limit for a TEXT column is theoretically unlimited but is bound by the space on the server.

Numeric Data Types

PostgreSQL supports several types of numeric data types, each of which has its own characteristics.

SMALLINT

A small integer is an integer value between the values of -32768 and +32767.

INTEGER

An integer is sometimes referred to as a "large integer". This data type can store values between -2147483648 and +2147483647.

BIGINT
A big integer can store values between -9223372036854775808 to +9223372036854775807.

SERIAL
A SERIAL column is the same size as the INTEGER but PostgreSQL automatically generates values into this type column. In other DBMS products this is often called an IDENTITY column because it is typically used to generate primary key values.

NUMERIC (also DECIMAL)
The NUMERIC type is defined with two numbers, one of which specifies the number of decimal positions and the other the number of those positions to the right of the decimal point. For example this value could be stored in a NUMERIC (7,2) column which specifies 7 total positions and 2 positions to the right of the decimal point:

```
10377.45
```

FLOAT
A DECFLOAT type means "decimal floating-point". The position of the decimal is stored with the value itself.

Date, time, and timestamp data types

Date/Time Types

DATE
The DATE type represents a date in year, month and day format. It is 10 bytes long and the format depends on the date format specified when PostgreSQL was installed. The default installation on PgAdmin uses the ASCII format which is:

```
YYYY-MM-DD (ISO standard)
```

TIME
The TIME type stores a time of day in hours, minutes and seconds. For example, 10:34 am and 27 seconds is:

```
10:34:27
```

TIMESTAMP
The TIMESTAMP type stores a value that represents both a date and a time. It includes

the year, month, date, hour, minute, seconds and microseconds. For example, the following timestamp is for April 17, 2017 at 02:17:54.

```
2017-04-17 02.17.54
```

XML data type
The XML data type defines a column that will store a well formed XML document. PostgreSQL provides a number of functions for manipulating the data stored in an XML column.

JSON
PostgreSQL provides two JSON data types: JSON and JSONB for storing JSON data. The JSON data type stores plain JSON data that requires reparsing for each processing, while JSONB data type stores JSON data in a binary format which is faster to process but slower to insert. In addition, JSONB supports indexing, which can be an advantage.

User Defined Type (UDT)
A UDT type is defined by the user and typically a refined version of a standard data type. UDT are at an intermediate level of difficulty, and will be covered in a later book for PostgreSQL intermediate topics.

Constraints

Types of constraints
There are basically four types of constraints, as follows:

1. Unique

2. Referential

3. Check

4. NULL

A UNIQUE constraint requires that the value in a particular field in a table be unique for each record.

A REFERENTIAL constraint enforces relationships between tables. For example you can define a referential constraint between an EMPLOYEE table and a DEPARTMENTS table, such that a DEPT field in the EMPLOYEE table can only contain a value that matches a key value in the DEPARTMENTS table.

A CHECK constraint establishes some condition on a column, such as the value must be >= 10.

A NOT NULL constraint establishes that each record must have a non-null value for this column.

Unique Constraints

A unique constraint is a rule that the values of a key are valid only if they are unique in a table. In the case of the EMPLOYEE table we have been working with, besides the primary index on EMP_ID, we created another unique index on the EMP_SSN as follows:

```
CREATE UNIQUE INDEX IDX_EMP_SSN ON EMPLOYEE (EMP_SSN);
```

Check Constraints

A check constraint is a rule that specifies the values that are allowed in one or more columns of every row of a base table. It establishes some condition on a column, such as the stored value must be >= 10. The real worth of check constraints is that business rules such as edits and validations can be stored in and performed by the database manager instead of application programs.

If you try to INSERT or UPDATE a record, the value in the column is evaluated against the check constraint rules. If the value follows the rules, then the action is permitted; otherwise the action will fail with a constraint violation.

Let's create a new table EMP_DATA, and then we'll define some check constraints on it. We'll create the table and then alter it to add the two constraints:

```
CREATE TABLE EMP_DATA
(EMP_ID INT PRIMARY KEY,
EMP_LNAME      VARCHAR(30),
EMP_FNAME      VARCHAR(20),
EMP_AGE INT);
```

Let's say we require that the employee number be a value between zero and 9999. Also the employee's age must be between 18 and 99. Now let's add the constraint on employee id.

```
ALTER TABLE EMP_DATA
ADD CONSTRAINT X_EMPID
CHECK (EMP_ID BETWEEN 0 AND 9999);
```

Next, we'll add the constraint on age.

```
ALTER TABLE EMP_DATA
ADD CONSTRAINT X_AGE
CHECK (EMP_AGE >= 18);
```

Now let's try this insert:

```
INSERT INTO EMP_DATA
VALUES
(17888,
'BROWN',
'WILLIAM',
17);

ERROR: new row for relation "emp_data" violates check constraint "x_age" DETAIL:
Failing row contains (17888, BROWN, WILLIAM, 17). SQL state: 23514
```

It turns out that we mis-keyed the employee id. It should be 1788 instead of 17888. The value 17888 exceeds 9999 which is the maximum limit for employee id according to the check constraint.

Let's fix the employee id and try again:

```
INSERT INTO EMP_DATA
VALUES
(1788,
'BROWN',
'WILLIAM',
17);

ERROR: new row for relation "emp_data" violates check constraint "x_age" DETAIL:
Failing row contains (1788, BROWN, WILLIAM, 17). SQL state: 23514
```

Obviously 17 is less than 18 which is the lower limit on the employee age. So let's fix the age and we can see the row is accepted now.

```
INSERT INTO EMP_DATA
VALUES
(1788,
'BROWN',
```

```
'WILLIAM',
18);
```

We can verify that the row was added.

Check constraints can be a very powerful way of building business logic into the database itself. No application programming is required to implement a constraint (other than trapping and handling violations). There is great consistency with using check constraints because the constraints are applied regardless of which program or ad hoc process attempts the data modification.

Referential Constraints

A referential constraint is the rule that the non-null values of a foreign key are valid only if they also appear as a key value in a parent table. The table that contains the parent key is called the parent table of the referential constraint, and the table that contains the foreign key is a dependent of that table. Referential constraints ensure data integrity by using primary and foreign key relationships between tables.

In PostgreSQL you define a referential constraint by specifying a column in the child table that references a primary key column in a parent table. For example, in a company you could have a DEPARTMENT table with column DEPT_CODE, and an EMP_DATA table that includes a column DEPT that represents the department code an employee is assigned to. The rule would be that you cannot have a value in the DEPT column of the EMP_DATA table that does not have a corresponding DEPT_CODE in the DEPARTMENT table. You can think of this as a parent and child relationship between the DEPARTMENT table and the EMP_DATA table.

Let's create the DEPARTMENT table and also add the DEPT column to the EMP_DATA table.

```
CREATE TABLE DEPARTMENT
(DEPT_CODE   CHAR (04) PRIMARY KEY,
DEPT_NAME    VARCHAR (20) NOT NULL);
```

Now let's add some data to the table.

```
INSERT INTO DEPARTMENT
VALUES ('DPTA','DEPARTMENT A');
```

Now let's alter our EMP_DATA table to add a DEPT column, and we'll set it to 'DPTA' for all rows.

```
ALTER TABLE EMP_DATA
ADD DEPT CHAR(04) REFERENCES DEPARTMENT (DEPT_CODE);

UPDATE EMP_DATA
SET DEPT = 'DPTA';
```

Now if you try to update an EMP_DATA record with a DEPT value that does not have a corresponding DEPT_CODE value in table DEPARTMENT, you'll get an SQL error indicating violation of a foreign key. Let's go ahead and try it:

```
UPDATE EMP_DATA
SET DEPT = 'DPTB';

ERROR: insert or update on table "emp_data" violates foreign key constraint
"emp_data_dept_fkey"  DETAIL:  Key  (dept)=(DPTB)  is  not  present  in  table
"department". SQL state: 23503
```

The parent table DEPARTMENT does not have EMP_DATA "DPTB" value in it, and our business rules (as implemented with a foreign key relationship) require that DPTB be added to the DEPARTMENT table before the EMP_DATA record can be updated with that value.

Deleting a Record from the Parent Table

Now let's talk about what happens if you want to delete a record from the parent table. Assuming no EMP_DATA records are linked to that DEPARTMENT record, deleting that record may be fine. But what if you are trying to delete a DEPARTMENT record who's EMP_DATA is referenced by one or more records in the EMP_DATA table?

Let's look at a record in the table:

```
SELECT EMP_ID, DEPT FROM EMP_DATA
WHERE EMP_ID = 1788;


EMP_ID DEPT
1788   DPTA
```

Ok, we know that the DEPT_CODE in use is DPTA. Now let's try to delete DPTA from the DEPARTMENT table.

```
DELETE FROM DEPARTMENT
WHERE DEPT_CODE = 'DPTA';

ERROR: update or delete on table "department" violates foreign key constraint
"emp_data_dept_fkey" on table "emp_data" DETAIL: Key (dept_code)=(DPTA) is still
referenced from table "emp_data". SQL state: 23503
```

60

As you can see, when we try to remove the DEPT_CODE from the DEPARTMENT table, we get a referential integrity violation. This one is telling us that our SQL is in violation of the referential constraint emp_data_dept_fkey. That's probably what we want, i.e., to have an error flagged. But there may be situation where you do not want to check for violations. In this case you could create the foreign key constraint using the WITH NO CHECK clause.

Not Null Constraints

A NOT NULL constraint on a column requires that when you add or update a record, you must specify a non null value for that column. If you do not specify a non null value, you will get an error. Let's take an example of trying update an EMPLOYEE record without specifying a value for one of the columns.

In this case, let's leave off the EMP_FIRST_NAME value which is defined in the table as NOT NULL.

```
INSERT INTO EMPLOYEE
(EMP_ID,
EMP_LAST_NAME,
EMP_PROMOTION_DATE)

VALUES (7420,
'JACKSON',
'2016-09-01');

ERROR: null value in column "emp_first_name" violates not-null constraint
DETAIL: Failing row contains (7420, JACKSON, null, 0, 2016-09-01, null). SQL
state: 23502
```

As expected, we get an error for not including a value for the EMP_FIRST_NAME column. Defining a column with the NOT NULL attribute ensures that no record can be added to the table with a NULL value in this column. The NOT NULL attribute enforces that requirement regardless of which application or user is processing the data, so it's "universal" and does not depend on program logic to enforce the business rule.

Identities

Some scenarios require an auto-generated number that can be used to uniquely identify a record. PostgreSQL provides a method of doing this by using an identity column. The identity column is so named because it allows you to uniquely identify a record, i.e., it provides a unique key. Let's do this example, and we'll create a different employee table for the example:

```
CREATE TABLE EMPLOYE2(
EMP_ID SMALLINT PRIMARY KEY GENERATED ALWAYS AS IDENTITY
(START WITH 1001 INCREMENT BY 1 NO CYCLE),
EMP_LAST_NAME VARCHAR(30) NOT NULL,
EMP_FIRST_NAME VARCHAR(20) NOT NULL,
EMP_SERVICE_YEARS INT NOT NULL DEFAULT 0,
EMP_PROMOTION_DATE DATE);
```

Now let's insert a row into the EMPLOYE2 table:

```
INSERT INTO EMPLOYE2
(EMP_LAST_NAME,
EMP_FIRST_NAME,
EMP_SERVICE_YEARS,
EMP_PROMOTION_DATE)
VALUES
('JOHNSON',
'BILL',
1,
'2016-12-01');
```

Notice that we did not specify any value for the EMP_ID. That is because EMP_ID is an identity field and PostgreSQL will generate the value. Now we can query the table and see the contents:

```
SELECT EMP_ID, EMP_LAST_NAME
FROM EMPLOYE2;
```

EMP_ID	EMP_LAST_NAME
1001	JOHNSON

Views

A view is a virtual table that is based on a SELECT query against a base table or another view. Views can include more than one table (or other view), including the results of a join.

DDL for Views

CREATE

The basic syntax to create a view is as follows:

```
CREATE VIEW <name of view> AS
SELECT <columns>
FROM <table>
WHERE <condition>
```

Optionally, you can specify the WITH CHECK OPTION. The WITH CHECK OPTION clause ensures that a record inserted via a view is consistent with the view definition. For example, let's go back to our EMPLOYE2 table. Let's say we want a view named EMP_SENIOR that shows us data from EMPLOYE2 only for senior employees, meaning employees with at least 5 years of service. We will also allow records to be inserted to the EMPLOYE2 table via the view. Here is the view definition:

```
CREATE VIEW EMP_SENIOR AS
SELECT EMP_ID,
EMP_LAST_NAME,
EMP_FIRST_NAME,
EMP_SERVICE_YEARS,
EMP_PROMOTION_DATE
FROM EMPLOYE2
WHERE EMP_SERVICE_YEARS >= 5;
```

Now let's insert a couple of records using this view.

```
INSERT INTO EMP_SENIOR
(EMP_LAST_NAME,
EMP_FIRST_NAME,
EMP_SERVICE_YEARS,
EMP_PROMOTION_DATE)
VALUES
('FORD',
'JAMES',
7,
'2015-01-01');
```

The first record we inserted is for an employee with more than 5 years of service. We can confirm that the record was successfully inserted by querying the view.

```
SELECT EMP_ID,
EMP_LAST_NAME,
EMP_FIRST_NAME
FROM EMP_SENIOR;
```

EMP_ID	EMP_LAST_NAME	EMP_FIRST_NAME
1002	FORD	JAMES

Now let's insert a record that does not fit the view definition. In this case, let's add a record for which the employee has only 2 years service:

```
INSERT INTO EMP_SENIOR
(EMP_LAST_NAME,
```

```
EMP_FIRST_NAME,
EMP_SERVICE_YEARS,
EMP_PROMOTION_DATE)
VALUES
('BUFORD',
'HOLLAND',
2,
'2016-07-31');
```

Interestingly, PostgreSQL allowed the record to be added to the table via the view even though the data did not match the view definition. We cannot know that fact from querying the view because when we do so it only shows us data which conforms to the view definition. Notice that only the record for the person with 7 years' service is returned by the view.

```
SELECT EMP_ID,
EMP_LAST_NAME,
EMP_FIRST_NAME
FROM EMP_SENIOR;


EMP_ID EMP_LAST_NAME EMP_FIRST_NAME
1002   FORD          JAMES
```

But when we query the base table, we see the new record was in fact added:

```
SELECT EMP_ID, EMP_LAST_NAME, EMP_FIRST_NAME
FROM EMPLOYEE;


EMP_ID EMP_LAST_NAME EMP_FIRST_NAME
1002   FORD          JAMES
1003   BUFORD        HOLLAND
1001   JOHNSON       BILL
```

Maybe this is ok if it fits your overall business rules. However, if you want to prevent records that do not conform to the view definition from being inserted into the table using that view, you must define the view using the WITH CHECK OPTION clause. Let's drop the view and recreate it that way.

```
DROP VIEW EMP_SENIOR;
COMMIT WORK;

CREATE VIEW EMP_SENIOR
AS
SELECT
EMP_ID,
EMP_LAST_NAME,
```

```
EMP_FIRST_NAME,
EMP_SERVICE_YEARS,
EMP_PROMOTION_DATE
FROM EMPLOYE2
WHERE EMP_SERVICE_YEARS >= 5
WITH CHECK OPTION;
```

Now let's try to insert two more records, first an employee with more 5 or more years of service.

```
INSERT INTO EMP_SENIOR
(EMP_LAST_NAME,
EMP_FIRST_NAME,
EMP_SERVICE_YEARS,
EMP_PROMOTION_DATE)
VALUES
('JACKSON',
'MARLO',
8,
'2015-06-30');
```

This still works which is fine. Now let's try one with less than 5 years of service. In this case the insert fails as we can see with a 3564 error code:

```
INSERT INTO EMP_SENIOR
(EMP_LAST_NAME,
EMP_FIRST_NAME,
EMP_SERVICE_YEARS,
EMP_PROMOTION_DATE)

VALUES
 ('TARKENTON',
'QUINCY',
3,
'2015-09-30');

ERROR: new row violates check option for view "emp_senior" DETAIL: Failing row
contains (1005, TARKENTON, QUINCY, 3, 2015-09-30). SQL state: 44000
```

This is how to create a view that will disallow any insert or update that does not conform to the view definition. This is one way of enforcing ever-changing business rules without changing the underlying table definition.

ALTER
Views cannot be changed. They must be dropped and recreated.

DROP

Finally, you can delete a view by issuing the DROP command.

```
DROP VIEW <view name>
```

Views for Security

For purposes of security, a view is a classic way to restrict a subset of data columns to a specific set of users who are allowed to see or manipulate those columns. If you are going to use views for security you must make sure that users do not have direct access to the base tables, i.e. that they can only access the data via view(s). Otherwise they could potentially circumvent your rules to allow only access by view.

Let's look back at our EMPLOYEE table. Suppose we add a column for the employee's Social Security number. That is obviously a very private piece of information that not everyone should see. Our business rule will be that users HRUSER01, HRUSER02 and HRUSER99 are the only ones who should be able to view Social Security numbers. All other users and/or groups are not allowed to see the content of this column, but they can access all the other columns.

We might implement this as follows, first verifying that we still have two rows with populated social security numbers:

```
SELECT EMP_ID, EMP_SSN
FROM EMPLOYEE;

EMP_ID  EMP_SSN
3217    123456789
7459    987654321
```

Now let's create two views, one of which includes the EMP_SSN column, and the other of which does not:

```
CREATE VIEW EMPLOYEE_ALL
AS SELECT
EMP_ID,
EMP_LAST_NAME,
EMP_FIRST_NAME,
EMP_SERVICE_YEARS,
EMP_PROMOTION_DATE
FROM EMPLOYEE;

CREATE VIEW EMPLOYEE_HR
AS SELECT
EMP_ID,
```

```
EMP_LAST_NAME,
EMP_FIRST_NAME,
EMP_SERVICE_YEARS,
EMP_PROMOTION_DATE,
EMP_SSN
FROM EMPLOYEE;
```

You would need to grant access to the EMPLOYEE_HR view for those users you want to be able to see the EMP_SSN value. All others can be granted access to the EMPLOYEE_ALL view which does not include the EMP_SSN column.

To prove this:

```
SELECT EMP_ID, EMP_SSN
FROM EMPLOYEE_ALL
WHERE EMP_ID = 3217;

ERROR: column "emp_ssn" does not exist LINE 1: SELECT EMP_ID, EMP_SSN ^ HINT:
Perhaps you meant to reference the column "employee_all.emp_id". SQL state:
42703 Character: 16
```

If you are one of the HR users who have access, you will be able to access the EMP_SSN column using the other view, EMPLOYEE_HR:

```
SELECT EMP_ID, EMP_SSN
FROM EMPLOYEE_HR
WHERE EMP_ID = 3217;
```

EMP_ID EMP_SSN
3217   123456789

Note that a view can reference another view. So we could create an EMPLOYEE_PAY view that includes a reference to the EMPLOYEE_ALL view.

Dropping the DBHR Database
As we conclude the DDL chapter of this textbook, I strongly recommend that you remove all the objects we have created thus far. This will enable us to begin with a clean slate for the next chapter on Data Manipulation Language. However, **if you want to do the chapter exercises on the following page, do those exercises first before you delete the database.**

The easiest way to remove all the database objects is to simply drop the database. You can do this in PgAdmin by running this:

```
SELECT pg_terminate_backend(pg_stat_activity.pid)
    FROM pg_stat_activity
    WHERE pg_stat_activity.datname = 'DBHR'
      AND pid <> pg_backend_pid();
```

Next execute this DDL:

```
DROP DATABASE "DBHR";
```

Chapter Two Exercises

1. Write a DDL statement to create a base table named EMP_DEPENDENT with schema DBHR. The columns should be named as follows and have the specified attributes. There is no primary key.

Field Name	Type	Attributes
EMP_ID	INTEGER	NOT NULL, PRIMARY KEY
EMP_DEP_LAST_NAME	VARCHAR(30)	NOT NULL
EMP_DEP_FIRST_NAME	VARCHAR(20)	NOT NULL
EMP_RELATIONSHIP	VARCHAR(15)	NOT NULL

2. Create a statement to create a referential constraint on table EMP_DEPENDENT such that only employee ids which exist on the EMPLOYEE table can have an entry in EMP_DEPENDENT. If there is an attempt to delete an EMPLOYEE record that has EMP_DEPENDENT records associated with it, then do not allow the delete to take place.

Chapter Three: Data Manipulation Language

Overview
Data Manipulation Language (DML) is used to add, change and delete data in a PostgreSQL table. DML is one of the most basic and essential skills you must have as a PostgreSQL professional. In this section we'll look at the five major DML statements: INSERT, UPDATE, DELETE and SELECT.

Setup for HR Database
In the previous chapter we created a database named DBHR. We dropped it so that we could start clean in this chapter. Your DBA will normally handle creating the database and other database objects, but if you are working by yourself on your own PC, you can reference these procedures.

Now create the DBHR database by right clicking the databases part of the postgreSQL tree, and selecting create new database and entering the DBHR database name. Alternately, you can enter the following DDL in the query window and execute it:

DML SQL Statements
Data Manipulation Language (DML) is at the core of working with relational databases. You need to be very comfortable with DML statements: INSERT, UPDATE, DELETE, MERGE and SELECT. We'll cover the syntax and use of each of these. For purposes of this section, let's plan and create a very simple table. Here are the columns and data types for our table which we will name EMPLOYEE.

Field Name	Type	Attributes
EMP_ID	INTEGER	NOT NULL, PRIMARY KEY, UNIQUE
EMP_LAST_NAME	VARCHAR(30)	NOT NULL
EMP_FIRST_NAME	VARCHAR(20)	NOT NULL
EMP_SERVICE_YEARS	INTEGER	NOT NULL, DEFAULT IS ZERO
EMP_PROMOTION_DATE	DATE	

The table can be created with the following DDL:

```
CREATE TABLE EMPLOYEE
(EMP_ID INT PRIMARY KEY,
EMP_LAST_NAME VARCHAR(30) NOT NULL,
EMP_FIRST_NAME VARCHAR(20) NOT NULL,
EMP_SERVICE_YEARS INT NOT NULL DEFAULT 0,
EMP_PROMOTION_DATE DATE);
```

71

INSERT Statement

The INSERT statement adds one or more rows to a table. There are two forms of the INSERT statement and you need to know the syntax of each of these.

- Insert via values
- Insert via select

Insert Via Values

There are actually two sub-forms of the insert by values. One form explicitly names the target fields and the other does not. Generally when inserting a record you explicitly name the target columns, followed by a VALUES clause that includes the actual values to apply to the columns in the new record. Let's use our EMPLOYEE table for this example:

```
INSERT INTO EMPLOYEE
(EMP_ID,
EMP_LAST_NAME,
EMP_FIRST_NAME,
EMP_SERVICE_YEARS,
EMP_PROMOTION_DATE)

VALUES (3217,
'JOHNSON',
'EDWARD',
4,
'2017-01-01');
```

A second sub-form of the INSERT statement via values is to omit the target fields and simply provide the VALUES clause. You can do this only if your values clause includes values for ALL the columns in the correct positional order.

Here's an example of this second sub-form of insert via values for the EMPLOYEE table:

```
INSERT INTO EMPLOYEE
VALUES (7459,
'STEWART',
'BETTY',
7,
'2016-07-31');
```

Note that EMP_ID is defined as a primary key on the table. If you try inserting a row for which the primary key already exists, you will receive a 2801 error code (meaning a record already exists with that key).

Another consideration for the INSERT statement concerns the use of the DEFAULT keyword. If you define a column with a default value using the DEFAULT clause, you can assign that default value to a record by simply specifying the word DEFAULT instead of an actual value in the INSERT statement.

Here's an example of specifying the DEFAULT value for the EMP_SERVICE_YEARS column, and the NULL value for the EMP_PROMOTION_DATE.

```
INSERT INTO EMPLOYEE
(EMP_ID,
EMP_LAST_NAME,
EMP_FIRST_NAME,
EMP_SERVICE_YEARS,
EMP_PROMOTION_DATE)

VALUES (9134,
'FRANKLIN',
'ROSEMARY',
DEFAULT,
NULL);
```

One final consideration concerns the use of the NULL value. If a column is not defined as NOT NULL (or if it is explicitly defined as NULL meaning NULL values are allowed), and you don't want to assign a value to that column, then you must specify NULL for the column in the values clause.

Before moving on to the Insert via Select option, let's take a look at the data we have in the table so far.

```
SELECT
EMP_ID,
EMP_LAST_NAME,
EMP_FIRST_NAME,
EMP_SERVICE_YEARS,
EMP_PROMOTION_DATE
FROM EMPLOYEE
ORDER BY EMP_ID;
```

EMP_ID	EMP_LAST_NAME	EMP_FIRST_NAME	EMP_SERVICE_YEARS	EMP_PROMOTION_DATE
3217	JOHNSON	EDWARD	4	2017-01-01
7459	STEWART	BETTY	7	2016-07-31
9134	FRANKLIN	ROSEMARY	0	[null]

Insert via Select

You can use a SELECT query to extract data from one table and load it to another. You can even include literals or built in functions in the SELECT query in lieu of column names (if you need them). This is often useful for loading tables. Let's do an example.

Suppose you have an employee recognition request table named EMPRECOG. This table is used to generate/store recognition requests for employees who have been promoted during a certain time frame. HR will print a recognition certificate and deliver it to the employee. Once the request is fulfilled, the date completed will be entered by HR in a separate process.

The table specification is as follows:

Field Name	Type	Attributes
EMP_ID	INTEGER	NOT NULL
EMP_PROMOTION_DATE	DATE	NOT NULL
EMP_RECOG_RQST_DATE	DATE	NOT NULL WITH DEFAULT
EMP_RECOG_COMP_DATE	DATE	

The DDL to create the table is as follows:

```
CREATE TABLE EMPRECOG
(EMP_ID INT NOT NULL,
EMP_PROMOTION_DATE DATE NOT NULL,
EMP_RECOG_RQST_DATE DATE
NOT NULL DEFAULT CURRENT_DATE,
EMP_RECOG_COMP_DATE DATE);
```

Your objective is to load this table with data from the EMPLOYEE table for any employee whose promotion date occurs during the current month. The selection criteria could be expressed as:

```
SELECT
EMP_ID,
EMP_PROMOTION_DATE
FROM EMPLOYEE
WHERE date_part('MONTH', EMP_PROMOTION_DATE)
    = date_part('MONTH', CURRENT_DATE);
```

To use this SQL in an INSERT statement on the EMPRECOG table, you would need to add a value for another column for the request date (EMP_RECOG_RQST_DATE). Let's use the CURRENT_DATE function to insert today's date as the requested date. Now our select statement looks like this:

74

```
SELECT
EMP_ID,
EMP_PROMOTION_DATE,
CURRENT_DATE AS RQST_DATE
FROM EMPLOYEE
WHERE date_part('MONTH', EMP_PROMOTION_DATE)
    = date_part('MONTH', CURRENT_DATE);
```

Assuming we are running the SQL on January 10, 2017 we should get the following results:

```
EMP_ID EMP_PROMOTION_DATE EMP_RECOG_RQST_DATE
3217   2017-01-01         2017-01-10
```

Let's create the INSERT statement for the EMPRECOG table. Since our query does not include the EMP_RQST_COMP_DATE (assume that the request complete column will be populated by another HR process when the request is complete), we must specify the target column names we are populating. Otherwise we will get a mismatch between the number of columns we are loading and the number in the table.

Of course, in circumstances where you have values for all the table's columns, you needn't include the column names and you can just use the INSERT INTO and SELECT statement. But in many cases it is handy to include the target column names, even when you don't have to. It makes the DML more self-documenting and helpful for the next developer.

Here is our SQL:

```
INSERT INTO EMPRECOG
(EMP_ID,
EMP_PROMOTION_DATE,
EMP_RECOG_RQST_DATE)
SELECT EMP_ID,
EMP_PROMOTION_DATE,
CURRENT_DATE AS RQST_DATE
FROM EMPLOYEE
WHERE date_part('MONTH', EMP_PROMOTION_DATE)
    = date_part('MONTH', CURRENT_DATE);
```

If you are following along and running the examples, you may notice it doesn't work if the real date is not a January 2017 date. You can make this one work by specifying the comparison date as 1/1/2017. So your query would be:

75

```
INSERT INTO EMPRECOG
(EMP_ID,
EMP_PROMOTION_DATE,
EMP_RECOG_RQST_DATE)
SELECT
EMP_ID,
EMP_PROMOTION_DATE,
'2017-01-10' AS RQST_DATE
FROM EMPLOYEE
WHERE date_part('MONTH', EMP_PROMOTION_DATE)
    = date_part('MONTH', DATE '2017-01-01');
```

After you run the SQL, query the EMPRECOG table, and you can see the result:

```
SELECT * FROM EMPRECOG;
```

EMP_ID	EMP_PROMOTION_DATE	EMP_RECOG_RQST_DATE	EMP_RECOG_COMP_DATE
3217	2017-01-01	2017-01-10	null

The above is what we expect. Only one of the employees has a promotion date in January, 2017. This employee has been added to the EMPRECOG table with request date of January 10 and a null recognition completed date.

Insert via Values for Multiple Rows
In PostgreSQL you can insert multiple sets of values in the VALUES clause on a single INSERT statement. You simply need to delimit the sets of values by the open and close parentheses, and use a comma between each set.

Let's look at an example.

```
INSERT INTO EMPLOYEE
(EMP_ID,
EMP_LAST_NAME,
EMP_FIRST_NAME,
EMP_SERVICE_YEARS,
EMP_PROMOTION_DATE)
VALUES (4720,
'SCHULTZ',
'TIM',
9,
'01/01/2017'),
(6288,
'WILLARD',
'JOE',
6,
'01/01/2016');
```

76

A brief query shows our current table data to be the following:

```
SELECT
EMP_ID,
EMP_LAST_NAME,
EMP_FIRST_NAME,
EMP_SERVICE_YEARS,
EMP_PROMOTION_DATE
FROM EMPLOYEE
ORDER BY EMP_ID;
```

EMP_ID	EMP_LAST_NAME	EMP_FIRST_NAME	EMP_SERVICE_YEARS	EMP_PROMOTION_DATE
3217	JOHNSON	EDWARD	4	2017-01-01
4720	SCHULTZ	TIM	9	2017-01-01
6288	WILLARD	JOE	6	2016-01-01
7459	STEWART	BETTY	7	2016-07-31
9134	FRANKLIN	ROSEMARY	0	null

Note: You can also INSERT to an underlying table via a view. The syntax is exactly the same as for inserting to a table.

UPDATE Statement

The UPDATE statement is pretty straightforward. It changes one or more records based on specified conditions. There are two forms of the UPDATE statement:

1. The searched update

2. The positioned update

The positioned update is used with a result set and we'll deal with that when we get to chapter five. Meanwhile let's look at the searched update.

The searched update is performed on records that meet a certain search criteria using a WHERE search clause. The basic form and syntax you need to know for the searched update is:

```
UPDATE <TABLENAME>
SET COLUMN NAME = <VALUE>
WHERE <CONDITION>
```

For example, recall that we left the promotion date for employee 9134 with a NULL value. Now let's say we want to update the promotion date to October 1, 2016. We could use this SQL to do that:

```
UPDATE EMPLOYEE
SET EMP_PROMOTION_DATE = '2016-10-01'
WHERE EMP_ID = 9134;
```

If you have more than one column to update, you must use a comma to separate the column names. For example, let's update both the promotion date and the first name of the employee. We'll make the first name Brianna and the promotion date 10/1/2016.

```
UPDATE EMPLOYEE
SET EMP_PROMOTION_DATE = '2016-10-01',
EMP_FIRST_NAME = 'BRIANNA'
WHERE EMP_ID = 9134;
```

Another sub-form of the UPDATE statement to be aware of is UPDATE without a WHERE clause. For example, to set the EMP_RECOG_COMP_DATE field to January 31, 2017 for every row in the EMPRECOG table, you could use this statement:

```
UPDATE EMPRECOG
SET EMP_RECOG_COMP_DATE = '2017-01-31';
```

Obviously you should be very careful using this form of UPDATE, as it will apply the value you specify for that column to every row in the table. This is normally not what you want, but it could be useful in cases where you need to initialize one or more columns for all rows of a relatively small table.

Let's do another example where we'll update multiple rows based on a condition. We need to specially set up test data for our example, so if you are following along, execute the following query:

```
UPDATE EMPLOYEE
SET EMP_LAST_NAME
   = LOWER(EMP_LAST_NAME)
WHERE EMP_LAST_NAME IN ('JOHNSON', 'STEWART', 'FRANKLIN');
```

Now here is the current content of our EMPLOYEE table:

```
SELECT EMP_ID, EMP_LAST_NAME, EMP_FIRST_NAME
FROM EMPLOYEE
ORDER BY EMP_ID;
```

EMP_ID	EMP_LAST_NAME	EMP_FIRST_NAME
3217	johnson	EDWARD
4720	SCHULTZ	TIM
6288	WILLARD	JOE

```
7459      stewart          BETTY
9134      franklin         BRIANNA
```

As you can see we have three last names that are in lower case. Assume that we have decided we want to store all names in upper case. We want to correct the lowercase data. We will check all records in the EMPLOYEE table and if the last name contains lower case, we want to change it to upper case.

To accomplish our objective we need only run a query using the UPPER function. We'll also only specify those rows for which the last name contains lower case letters. Put another way, we only want to apply the update to those rows that actually need to be changed.

Here is our update query:

```
UPDATE EMPLOYEE
SET EMP_LAST_NAME = UPPER(EMP_LAST_NAME)
WHERE EMP_LAST_NAME <> UPPER(EMP_LAST_NAME);
```

And here is the modified data in the table:

```
SELECT EMP_ID, EMP_LAST_NAME,
EMP_FIRST_NAME FROM EMPLOYEE
ORDER BY EMP_ID;
```

EMP_ID	EMP_LAST_NAME	EMP_FIRST_NAME
3217	JOHNSON	EDWARD
4720	SCHULTZ	TIM
6288	WILLARD	JOE
7459	STEWART	BETTY
9134	FRANKLIN	BRIANNA

DELETE Statement

The DELETE statement is also pretty straightforward. It removes one or more records from the table based on specified conditions. As with the UPDATE statement, there are two forms of the DELETE statement:

1. The searched delete

2. The positioned delete

And as with the UPDATE statement, the positioned delete is used with a result set and we'll deal with that when we get to chapter five. Meanwhile let's look at the searched delete.

Searched DELETE

The searched delete is performed on records that meet a certain criteria, i.e., based on a WHERE clause. The basic form and syntax you need to remember for the searched DELETE is:

```
DELETE FROM <TABLENAME> WHERE <CONDITION>
```

For example, we might want to remove the record with employee id 9134. We could use this SQL to do that:

```
DELETE FROM EMPLOYEE WHERE EMP_ID = 9134;
```

Let's add this employee back to the table so it will be available for a later example.

```
INSERT INTO EMPLOYEE
(EMP_ID,
EMP_LAST_NAME,
EMP_FIRST_NAME,
EMP_SERVICE_YEARS,
EMP_PROMOTION_DATE)

VALUES (9134,
'FRANKLIN',
'BRIANNA',
DEFAULT,
NULL);
```

Now let's do another example of the searched delete. Suppose we want to delete any employee record which does not have a promotion date. Checking our data, we find a single row lacks a promotion date (sorry Brianna!).

```
SELECT EMP_ID,
EMP_LAST_NAME,
EMP_FIRST_NAME,
EMP_PROMOTION_DATE
FROM EMPLOYEE;
```

EMP_ID	EMP_LAST_NAME	EMP_FIRST_NAME	EMP_PROMOTION_DATE
9134	FRANKLIN	BRIANNA	null
7459	STEWART	BETTY	2016-07-31
4720	SCHULTZ	TIM	2017-01-01
3217	JOHNSON	EDWARD	2017-01-01
6288	WILLARD	JOE	2016-01-01

Our delete SQL would look like this:

```
DELETE FROM EMPLOYEE
WHERE EMP_PROMOTION_DATE IS NULL;
```

A single row was deleted from the table, as we can confirm by querying EMPLOYEE:

```
SELECT EMP_ID,
EMP_PROMOTION_DATE
FROM EMPLOYEE
ORDER BY EMP_ID;
```

EMP_ID	EMP_PROMOTION_DATE
3217	2017-01-01
4720	2017-01-01
6288	2016-01-01
7459	2016-07-31

Ok let's add Brianna back to the table.

```
INSERT INTO EMPLOYEE
(EMP_ID,
EMP_LAST_NAME,
EMP_FIRST_NAME,
EMP_SERVICE_YEARS,
EMP_PROMOTION_DATE)

VALUES (9134,
'FRANKLIN',
'BRIANNA',
DEFAULT,
'2016-10-01');
```

Finally, another sub-form of the DELETE statement to be aware of is the DELETE without a WHERE clause. For example, to remove all records from the EMPRECOG table, use this statement:

```
DELETE FROM EMPRECOG;
```

Be very careful using this form of DELETE, as it will remove every record from the target table. This is normally not what you want, but it could be useful in cases where you need to initialize a relatively small table to empty.

INSERT ON CONFLICT DO UPDATE Statement

There is no MERGE statement in PostgreSQL, but you can use a variant which is:

```
INSERTON CONFLICT DO UPDATE
```

So what problem does the INSERT ON CONFLICT DO UPDATE solve? It adds/updates records for a table from a data source when you don't know whether the row already exists in the target table or not. An example could be if you are updating data in your table based on a flat file you receive from another system, department or even another company. Assuming the other system does not send you an action code (add, change or delete), you won't know whether to use the INSERT or UPDATE statement.

One way of handling this situation is to first try doing an INSERT and if you get a - 803 SQL error code, then you know the record already exists. In that case you would need to do an UPDATE instead. Or you could first try doing an UPDATE and then if you received an SQLCODE +100, you would know the record does not exist and you would do an INSERT. This solution works, but it inevitably wastes some PostgreSQL calls.

A more elegant solution is the INSERT ON CONFLICT DO UPDATE statement. We'll look at an example of this below. You'll notice the example is a pretty long SQL statement, but don't be put off by that. The SQL is only slightly longer than the combined INSERT and UPDATE statements you would have used otherwise.

Single Row Merge Using Hardcoded Values

Let's do an example. Let's say we want to merge data for employee Deborah Jenkins' into the EMPLOYEE table. Assume this information is being fed to us from another system which also supplied the EMP_ID, but we don't know whether that EMP_ID already exists in our EMPLOYEE table or not. So let's use the INSERT ON CONFLICT DO UPDATE statement:

Here is the SQL to do this. Note that the existing EMPLOYEE table is given with a T qualifier and the new information is given with S as the qualifier (these qualifiers are arbitrary – you can use any tag you want). We are matching the new information to the table based on employee id. When the insert is attempted, the data in the VALUES clause is used to create a new record. On the other hand, if the key value already exists, the data from the values clause is used to update the record. Note the use of the table name EXCLUDED refers to the data that was not inserted to the table.

```
INSERT INTO EMPLOYEE AS T
(EMP_ID,
 EMP_LAST_NAME,
```

```
        EMP_FIRST_NAME,
        EMP_SERVICE_YEARS,
        EMP_PROMOTION_DATE)
VALUES (1122,
'JENKINS',
'DEBORAH',
5,
NULL)

ON CONFLICT (EMP_ID) DO UPDATE
SET EMP_LAST_NAME = EXCLUDED.EMP_LAST_NAME,
    EMP_FIRST_NAME      = EXCLUDED.EMP_FIRST_NAME,
    EMP_SERVICE_YEARS  = EXCLUDED.EMP_SERVICE_YEARS,
    EMP_PROMOTION_DATE = EXCLUDED.EMP_PROMOTION_DATE
    WHERE T.EMP_ID  = EXCLUDED.EMP_ID;
```

Now let's examine the contents of our EMPLOYEE table:

```
SELECT * FROM EMPLOYEE ORDER BY EMP_ID;
```

EMP_ID	EMP_LAST_NAME	EMP_FIRST_NAME	EMP_SERVICE_YEARS	EMP_PROMOTION_DATE
1122	JENKINS	DEBORAH	5	null
3217	JOHNSON	EDWARD	4	2017-01-01
4720	SCHULTZ	TIM	9	2017-01-01
6288	WILLARD	JOE	6	2016-01-01
7459	STEWART	BETTY	7	2016-07-31
9134	FRANKLIN	BRIANNA	0	2016-10-01

As you can see, Ms. Jenkins is now in the EMPLOYEE table. I'll leave it to you for an exercise to use this same technicque to update a record where the row already exists in the table.

This is a trivial example but it shows how we can apply hardcoded data to the table when we don't know whether the employee already has an entry or not. This is handy for merging a single record.

Now let's continue with an example where we have multiple updates to apply to a table – some are new rows to add and some are for update of existing rows.

INSERT ON CONFLICT DO UPDATE With Two Tables
Let's now look at how we can merge multiple records between two tables, some of which exist in the target table and some of which do not. Again we will use the INSERT ON CONFLICT DO UPDATE statement.

Let's create a table that includes pay information for the employees defined as EMP_PAY. It will include the base and bonus pay for each employee identified by employee id. Here are the columns we need to define.

Field Name	Type	Attributes
EMP_ID	INTEGER	NOT NULL, PRIMARY KEY
EMP_REGULAR_PAY	DECIMAL	NOT NULL
EMP_BONUS	DECIMAL	

The DDL would look like this:

```
CREATE TABLE EMP_PAY
(EMP_ID INT PRIMARY KEY,
EMP_REGULAR_PAY DECIMAL (8,2) NOT NULL,
EMP_BONUS_PAY DECIMAL (8,2));
```

Next, let's add three records:

```
INSERT INTO EMP_PAY
VALUES (3217, 80000.00, 4000);

INSERT INTO EMP_PAY
VALUES (7459, 80000.00, 4000);

INSERT INTO EMP_PAY
VALUES (9134, 70000.00, NULL);
```

Now the current data in the table is as follows:

```
SELECT * FROM EMP_PAY ORDER BY EMP_ID;
```

EMP_ID	EMP_REGULAR_PAY	EMP_BONUS_PAY
3217	80000	4000
7459	80000	4000
9134	70000	null

OK, now let's assume we have a feed of data from another system that is stored in a table named EMP_PAY_TEMP which is identical in structure to EMP_PAY. Let's create this table as follows:

```
CREATE TABLE EMP_PAY_TEMP
(EMP_ID INT PRIMARY KEY,
EMP_REGULAR_PAY DECIMAL (8,2) NOT NULL,
EMP_BONUS_PAY DECIMAL (8,2));
```

84

Now let's add some records to it:

```
INSERT INTO EMP_PAY_TEMP
VALUES (3217, 65000.00, 5500.00);

INSERT INTO EMP_PAY_TEMP
VALUES (4720, 80000.00, 2500.00);

INSERT INTO EMP_PAY_TEMP
VALUES (6288, 70000.00, 2000.00);

INSERT INTO EMP_PAY_TEMP
VALUES (7459, 85000.00, 4000.00);

INSERT INTO EMP_PAY_TEMP
VALUES (9134, 75000.00, 2500.00);
```

And here is the data in our EMP_PAY_TEMP table.

```
SELECT * FROM EMP_PAY_TEMP;
```

EMP_ID	EMP_REGULAR_PAY	EMP_BONUS_PAY
9134	75000	2500
7459	85000	4000
4720	80000	2500
3217	65000	5500
6288	70000	2000

Looking at this data we know that our INSERT ON CONFLICT DO UPDATE will need to update three records that are already on the table, and it will add two records that don't currently exist on the table (EMP_IDs 4720 and 6288).

Here is our query which will merge the EMP_PAY_TEMP data into EMP_PAY.

```
INSERT INTO EMP_PAY AS T
(EMP_ID, EMP_REGULAR_PAY, EMP_BONUS_PAY)
SELECT EMP_ID, EMP_REGULAR_PAY, EMP_BONUS_PAY
FROM EMP_PAY_TEMP

ON CONFLICT (EMP_ID) DO UPDATE
SET EMP_REGULAR_PAY  = EXCLUDED.EMP_REGULAR_PAY,
    EMP_BONUS_PAY    = EXCLUDED. EMP_BONUS_PAY
    WHERE T.EMP_ID   = EXCLUDED.EMP_ID;
```

And now we can verify that the results were actually applied to the table.

```
SELECT * FROM EMP_PAY ORDER BY EMP_ID;
```

EMP_ID	EMP_REGULAR_PAY	EMP_BONUS_PAY
3217	65000	5500
4720	80000	2500
6288	70000	2000
7459	85000	4000
9134	75000	2500

The power of the INSERT ON CONFLICT DO UPDATE statement is that you do not need to know whether a record already exists when you apply the data to the table. The program logic is simplified – there is no trial and error to determine whether or not the record exists.

SELECT Statement

SELECT is the main statement you will use to retrieve data from a table or view.

The basic syntax for the select statement is:

```
SELECT  <column names>
FROM    <table or view name>
WHERE   <condition>
ORDER BY      <column name or number to sort by>
```

Let's return to our EMPLOYEE table for an example:

```
SELECT EMP_ID, EMP_LAST_NAME, EMP_FIRST_NAME
FROM EMPLOYEE
WHERE EMP_ID = 3217;
```

EMP_ID	EMP_LAST_NAME	EMP_FIRST_NAME
3217	JOHNSON	EDWARD

You can also change the column heading on the result set by specifying <column name> AS <literal>. For example:

```
SELECT EMP_ID AS "EMPLOYEE NUMBER",
EMP_LAST_NAME AS "EMPLOYEE LAST NAME",
EMP_FIRST_NAME AS "EMPLOYEE FIRST NAME"
FROM EMPLOYEE
WHERE EMP_ID = 3217;
```

EMPLOYEE NUMBER	EMPLOYEE LAST NAME	EMPLOYEE FIRST NAME
3217	JOHNSON	EDWARD

Now let's look at some clauses that will further qualify the rows that are returned.

WHERE CONDITION

There are quite a lot of options for the WHERE condition. In fact, you can use multiple where conditions by specifying AND and OR clauses. Be aware of the equality operators which are:

= Equal to
<> Not equal to
> Greater than
>= Greater than or equal to
< Less than
<= Less than or equal to

Let's look at some examples of WHERE conditions.

OR

```
SELECT EMP_ID,
EMP_LAST_NAME,
EMP_FIRST_NAME
FROM EMPLOYEE
WHERE EMP_ID = 3217 OR EMP_ID = 9134;
```

EMP_ID	EMP_LAST_NAME	EMP_FIRST_NAME
9134	FRANKLIN	BRIANNA
3217	JOHNSON	EDWARD

AND

```
SELECT EMP_ID,
EMP_LAST_NAME,
EMP_FIRST_NAME,
EMP_PROMOTION_DATE
FROM EMPLOYEE
WHERE (EMP_SERVICE_YEARS > 1)
AND (EMP_PROMOTION_DATE > '2016-12-31');
```

EMP_ID	EMP_LAST_NAME	EMP_FIRST_NAME	EMP_PROMOTION_DATE
4720	SCHULTZ	TIM	2017-01-01
3217	JOHNSON	EDWARD	2017-01-01

IN

You can specify that the column value must be present in a specified collection of values, either those you code in the SQL explicitly or a collection that is a result of a query. Let's look at an example of specifying specific EMP_ID values as a set.

```
SELECT EMP_ID,
EMP_LAST_NAME,
EMP_FIRST_NAME
FROM EMPLOYEE
WHERE EMP_ID IN (3217, 9134);
```

EMP_ID	EMP_LAST_NAME	EMP_FIRST_NAME
9134	FRANKLIN	BRIANNA
3217	JOHNSON	EDWARD

Now let's provide a listing of employees who are in the EMPLOYEE table but who are NOT in the EMP_PAY table yet. This example shows us two new techniques, use of the NOT keyword and use of a subselect query to create a collection result set. First, let's add a couple of records to the EMPLOYEE table:

```
INSERT INTO EMPLOYEE
(EMP_ID,
EMP_LAST_NAME,
EMP_FIRST_NAME,
EMP_SERVICE_YEARS,
EMP_PROMOTION_DATE)
VALUES (3333,
'FORD',
'JAMES',
7,
'2015-10-01');

INSERT INTO EMPLOYEE
(EMP_ID,
EMP_LAST_NAME,
EMP_FIRST_NAME,
EMP_SERVICE_YEARS,
EMP_PROMOTION_DATE)
VALUES (7777,
'HARRIS',
'ELISA',
2,
NULL);
```

Now let's run our mismatch query:

```
SELECT EMP_ID,
EMP_LAST_NAME,
EMP_FIRST_NAME
FROM EMPLOYEE
WHERE EMP_ID
NOT IN (SELECT EMP_ID FROM EMP_PAY);
```

EMP_ID	EMP_LAST_NAME	EMP_FIRST_NAME
7777	HARRIS	ELISA
1122	JENKINS	DEBORAH
3333	FORD	JAMES

Our results show those records in the EMPLOYEE table that have no corresponding records in the EMP_PAY table.

Incidentally, you can also use the EXCEPT predicate to identify rows in one table that have no counterpart in the other. For example, suppose we want the employee ids of any employee who has not received a paycheck. You could quickly identify them with this SQL:

```
SELECT EMP_ID
FROM EMPLOYEE
EXCEPT (SELECT EMP_ID FROM EMP_PAY);
```

EMP_ID
1122
3333
7777

One limitation of the EXCEPT clause is that the columns in the two queries have to match exactly, so you could not bring back a column from EMPLOYEE that does not also exist in the EMP_PAY table. Still the EXCEPT is useful in some cases, especially where you need to identify discrepancies between tables using a single column.

BETWEEN

The BETWEEN clause allows you to specify a range of values inclusive of the start and end value you provide. Here's an example where we want to retrieve the employee id and pay rate for all employees whose pay rate is between 60,000 and 85,000 annually.

```
SELECT EMP_ID,
EMP_REGULAR_PAY
FROM EMP_PAY
WHERE EMP_REGULAR_PAY BETWEEN 60000 AND 85000;
```

```
EMP_ID  EMP_REGULAR_PAY
9134    75000
7459    85000
4720    80000
3217    65000
6288    70000
```

LIKE

You can use the LIKE predicate to select values that match a pattern. For example, let's choose all rows for which the last name begins with the letter B. The % character is used as a wild card for any string value or character. So in this case we are retrieving every record for which the EMP_FIRST_NAME starts with the letter B.

```
SELECT EMP_ID,
EMP_LAST_NAME,
EMP_FIRST_NAME
FROM EMPLOYEE
WHERE EMP_FIRST_NAME LIKE 'B%';
```

```
EMP_ID  EMP_LAST_NAME   EMP_FIRST_NAME
9134    FRANKLIN        BRIANNA
7459    STEWART         BETTY
```

LIMIT

You can limit your result set by using the LIMIT clause with a number. For example, suppose you just want the employee id and names of any three records from the employee table. You can code it as follows:

```
SELECT EMP_ID,
EMP_LAST_NAME,
EMP_FIRST_NAME
FROM EMPLOYEE
LIMIT 3;
```

```
EMP_ID  EMP_LAST_NAME   EMP_FIRST_NAME
4720    SCHULTZ         TIM
6288    WILLARD         JOE
3217    JOHNSON         EDWARD
```

DISTINCT

Use the DISTINCT operator when you want to eliminate duplicate values. To illustrate this, let's create a couple of new tables. The first is called EMP_PAY_CHECK and we will use to store a calculated bi-monthly pay amount for each employee based on their annual salary. The DDL to create EMP_PAY_CHECK is a s follows:

90

```
CREATE TABLE EMP_PAY_CHECK
(EMP_ID INT NOT NULL,
EMP_REGULAR_PAY DECIMAL (8,2) NOT NULL,
EMP_SEMIMTH_PAY DECIMAL (8,2) NOT NULL);
```

Now let's insert some data into the EMP_PAY_CHECK table by calculating a twice monthly pay check:

```
INSERT INTO EMP_PAY_CHECK
SELECT EMP_ID,
EMP_REGULAR_PAY,
EMP_REGULAR_PAY / 24 FROM EMP_PAY;
```

Let's look at the results:

```
SELECT *
FROM EMP_PAY_CHECK
ORDER BY EMP_ID;
```

EMP_ID	EMP_REGULAR_PAY	EMP_SEMIMTH_PAY
3217	65000	2708.33
4720	80000	3333.33
6288	70000	2916.67
7459	85000	3541.67
9134	75000	3125

We now know how much each employee should make in their pay check. The next step is to create a history table of each pay check the employee receives. First we'll create the table and then we'll load it with data.

```
CREATE TABLE EMP_PAY_HIST
(EMP_ID INT NOT NULL,
EMP_PAY_DATE   DATE NOT NULL,
EMP_PAY_AMT    DECIMAL (8,2) NOT NULL);
```

Now let's add some records to it.

```
INSERT INTO EMP_PAY_HIST
SELECT EMP_ID,
'2017-01-15',
EMP_SEMIMTH_PAY
FROM EMP_PAY_CHECK;

INSERT INTO EMP_PAY_HIST
SELECT EMP_ID,
'2017-01-31',
```

```
    EMP_SEMIMTH_PAY
FROM EMP_PAY_CHECK;

INSERT INTO EMP_PAY_HIST
SELECT EMP_ID,
'2017-02-15',
EMP_SEMIMTH_PAY
FROM EMP_PAY_CHECK;

INSERT INTO EMP_PAY_HIST
SELECT EMP_ID,
'2017-02-28',
EMP_SEMIMTH_PAY
FROM EMP_PAY_CHECK;
```

Now we can look at the history table content which is as follows:

```
SELECT * FROM EMP_PAY_HIST;
```

EMP_ID	EMP_PAY_DATE	EMP_PAY_AMT
3217	2017-01-15	2708.33
3217	2017-01-31	2708.33
3217	2017-02-15	2708.33
3217	2017-02-28	2708.33
4720	2017-01-15	3333.33
4720	2017-01-31	3333.33
4720	2017-02-15	3333.33
4720	2017-02-28	3333.33
6288	2017-01-15	2916.67
6288	2017-01-31	2916.67
6288	2017-02-15	2916.67
6288	2017-02-28	2916.67
7459	2017-01-15	3541.67
7459	2017-01-31	3541.67
7459	2017-02-15	3541.67
7459	2017-02-28	3541.67
9134	2017-01-15	3125
9134	2017-01-31	3125
9134	2017-02-15	3125
9134	2017-02-28	3125

If you want a list of all employees who got a paycheck during the month of February, you would need to eliminate the duplicate entries because there are two for each employee. You could accomplish that with this SQL:

```
SELECT DISTINCT EMP_ID
FROM EMP_PAY_HIST
WHERE date_part('MONTH', EMP_PAY_DATE) = '02'
```

```
ORDER BY EMP_ID;

EMP_ID
3217
4720
6288
7459
9134
```

The DISTINCT operator ensures that only unique records are selected based on the columns you are returning. This is important because if you included additional columns in the results, any value that makes the record unique will also make it NOT a duplicate.

For example, let's add the payment date to our query and see the results:

```
SELECT DISTINCT EMP_ID, EMP_PAY_DATE
FROM EMP_PAY_HIST
WHERE date_part('MONTH', EMP_PAY_DATE) = '02'
ORDER BY EMP_ID;

EMP_ID  EMP_PAY_DATE
3217    2017-02-28
3217    2017-02-15
4720    2017-02-15
4720    2017-02-28
6288    2017-02-15
6288    2017-02-28
7459    2017-02-15
7459    2017-02-28
9134    2017-02-28
9134    2017-02-15
```

Since the combination of the employee id and payment date makes each record unique, you'll get multiple rows for each employee. So you must be careful in using DISTINCT to ensure that the structure of your query is really what you want.

SUBQUERY

A subquery is essentially a query within a query. Suppose for example we want to list the employee or employees who make the largest salary in the company. You can use a subquery to determine the maximum salary, and then use that value in the WHERE clause of your main query.

```
SELECT EMP_ID, EMP_REGULAR_PAY
FROM EMP_PAY
WHERE EMP_REGULAR_PAY
= (SELECT MAX(EMP_REGULAR_PAY) FROM EMP_PAY);
```

```
EMP_ID    EMP_REGULAR_PAY
7459      85000
```

What if there is more than one employee who makes the highest salary? Let's bump employee 9134 up to 85000 (and 4500 bonus) and see.

```
UPDATE EMP_PAY
SET EMP_REGULAR_PAY = 85000.00,
EMP_BONUS_PAY = 4500
WHERE EMP_ID = 9134;
```

Now let's see if our subquery still works:

```
SELECT EMP_ID, EMP_REGULAR_PAY
FROM EMP_PAY
WHERE EMP_REGULAR_PAY
  = (SELECT MAX(EMP_REGULAR_PAY) FROM EMP_PAY);


EMP_ID EMP_REGULAR_PAY
9134   85000
7459   85000
```

And in fact the query pulls both of the employees who earn the top pay. Subqueries are very powerful in that any value you can produce via a subquery can be substituted into a main query as selection criteria.

GROUP BY

You can summarize data using the GROUP BY clause. For example, let's determine how many distinct employee salary rates there are and how many employees are paid those amounts. As you can see, there are 4 groups.

```
SELECT EMP_REGULAR_PAY,
COUNT(*) AS "HOW MANY"
FROM EMP_PAY
GROUP BY EMP_REGULAR_PAY;

EMP_REGULAR_PAY        HOW MANY
80000                 1
85000                 2
65000                 1
70000                 1
```

ORDER BY

You can sort the display into ascending or descending sequence using the ORDER BY clause. To take the query we were just using for the group-by, let's present the data in descending sequence:

```
SELECT EMP_REGULAR_PAY,
COUNT(*)
AS "HOW MANY"
FROM EMP_PAY
GROUP BY
EMP_REGULAR_PAY
ORDER BY
EMP_REGULAR_PAY DESC;
```

EMP_REGULAR_PAY	HOW MANY
85000	2
80000	1
70000	1
65000	1

HAVING

You could also use the GROUP BY with a HAVING clause that limits the results to only those groups that meet another condition. Let's specify that the group must have more than one employee in it to be included in the results.

```
SELECT EMP_REGULAR_PAY,
COUNT(*) AS "HOW MANY"
FROM EMP_PAY
GROUP BY EMP_REGULAR_PAY
HAVING COUNT(*) > 1
ORDER BY EMP_REGULAR_PAY DESC;
```

EMP_REGULAR_PAY	HOW MANY
85000	2

Or if you want pay rates that have only one employee you could specify the count 1.

```
SELECT EMP_REGULAR_PAY,
COUNT(*) AS "HOW MANY"
FROM EMP_PAY
GROUP BY EMP_REGULAR_PAY
HAVING COUNT(*) = 1
ORDER BY EMP_REGULAR_PAY DESC;
```

EMP_REGULAR_PAY	HOW MANY
80000	1

```
70000                    1
65000                    1
```

Before we move on, let's reset our employee to whom we gave a temporary raise.

Otherwise our EMP_PAY and EMP_PAY_CHECK tables will not be in sync.

```
UPDATE EMP_PAY
SET EMP_REGULAR_PAY = 75000.00,
EMP_BONUS_PAY = 2500
WHERE EMP_ID = 9134;
```

Now our EMP_PAY table is restored:

```
SELECT * FROM EMP_PAY;
```

EMP_ID	EMP_REGULAR_PAY	EMP_BONUS_PAY
3217	65000	5500
4720	80000	2500
6288	70000	2000
7459	85000	4000
9134	75000	2500

CASE Expressions

In some situations you may need to code rather complex conditional logic into your queries. Assume we have a requirement to report all employees according to seniority. Report those who have less than a year service as ENTRY, employees who have a year or more service but less than 5 years as ADVANCED, and all employees with 5 years or more service as SENIOR. Here is a sample query that performs this using a CASE expression:

```
SELECT EMP_ID,
EMP_LAST_NAME,
EMP_FIRST_NAME,
CASE
WHEN EMP_SERVICE_YEARS    < 1 THEN 'ENTRY'
WHEN EMP_SERVICE_YEARS    < 5 THEN 'ADVANCED'
ELSE 'SENIOR'
END
FROM EMPLOYEE;
```

EMP_ID	EMP_LAST_NAME	EMP_FIRST_NAME	EMP_SERVICE_YEARS
9134	FRANKLIN	BRIANNA	ENTRY
1122	JENKINS	DEBORAH	SENIOR
4720	SCHULTZ	TIM	SENIOR

96

7459	STEWART	BETTY	SENIOR
3217	JOHNSON	EDWARD	ADVANCED
3333	FORD	JAMES	SENIOR
7777	HARRIS	ELISA	ADVANCED
6288	WILLARD	JOE	SENIOR

You'll notice that the column heading for the case result is `EMP_SERVICE_YEARS` which is a default based on the fact that we are evaluating that column. If you want to use another name such as "level", then instead of closing the CASE statement with just END, close it with END AS <some literal>. So if we want to call the result of the CASE expression an employee's "LEVEL", code it this way:

```
SELECT EMP_ID,
EMP_LAST_NAME,
EMP_FIRST_NAME,
CASE
WHEN EMP_SERVICE_YEARS     < 1 THEN 'ENTRY'
WHEN EMP_SERVICE_YEARS     < 5 THEN 'ADVANCED'
ELSE 'SENIOR' END AS LEVEL
FROM EMPLOYEE;
```

EMP_ID	EMP_LAST_NAME	EMP_FIRST_NAME	LEVEL
9134	FRANKLIN	BRIANNA	ENTRY
1122	JENKINS	DEBORAH	SENIOR
4720	SCHULTZ	TIM	SENIOR
7459	STEWART	BETTY	SENIOR
3217	JOHNSON	EDWARD	ADVANCED
3333	FORD	JAMES	SENIOR
7777	HARRIS	ELISA	ADVANCED
6288	WILLARD	JOE	SENIOR

JOINS

Now let's look at some cases where we need to extract data from more than one table. To do this we can use a join. Before we start running queries I want to add one row to the `EMP_PAY_CHECK` table. This is needed to make some of the joins work later, so bear with me.

```
INSERT INTO EMP_PAY_CHECK
VALUES
(7033,
77000.00,
77000 / 24);
```

Now our `EMP_PAY_CHECK` table now has these rows.

```
SELECT * FROM EMP_PAY_CHECK ORDER BY EMP_ID;
```

EMP_ID	EMP_REGULAR_PAY	EMP_SEMIMTH_PAY
3217	65000	2708.33
4720	80000	3333.33
6288	70000	2916.67
7033	77000	3208
7459	85000	3541.67
9134	75000	3125

Inner Joins

An inner join combines each row of one table with each row of the other table, keeping only the rows in which the join condition is true. You can join more than two tables but keep in mind that the more tables you join, the more record I/O is required and this could be a performance consideration. When I say a "performance consideration" I do not mean it is necessarily a problem. I mean it is one factor of many to keep in mind when designing an application process.

Let's do an example. Assume we want a report that includes employee id, first and last names and pay rate for each employee. To accomplish this we need data from both the EMPLOYEE and the EMP_PAY tables. We can match the tables on EMP_ID which is the column they have in common.

We can perform our join either implicitly or with the JOIN verb (explicitly). The first example will perform the join implicitly by specifying we will only include rows for which the EMPLOYEE in the EMPLOYEE table matches the EMP_ID in the EMP_PAY table.

```
SELECT A.EMP_ID,
A.EMP_LAST_NAME,
A.EMP_FIRST_NAME,
B.EMP_REGULAR_PAY
FROM EMPLOYEE A, EMP_PAY B
WHERE A.EMP_ID = B.EMP_ID
ORDER BY A.EMP_ID;
```

EMP_ID	EMP_LAST_NAME	EMP_FIRST_NAME	EMP_REGULAR_PAY
3217	JOHNSON	EDWARD	65000
4720	SCHULTZ	TIM	80000
6288	WILLARD	JOE	70000
7459	STEWART	BETTY	85000
9134	FRANKLIN	BRIANNA	75000

Notice that in the SQL the column names are prefixed with a tag that is associated with the table being referenced. This is needed in all cases where the column being referenced exists in both tables with the same column name. If you do not specify the tag, you will get an error that your column name reference is ambiguous, i.e., PostgreSQL does not know which table you are referencing when you refer to a column.

Moving on, you can use an explicit join by specifying the JOIN or INNER JOIN verbs. This is actually a best practice because it helps keep the query clearer for those developers who follow you, especially as your queries get more complex.

```
SELECT A.EMP_ID,
A.EMP_LAST_NAME,
A.EMP_FIRST_NAME,
B.EMP_REGULAR_PAY
FROM EMPLOYEE A
INNER JOIN
EMP_PAY B
ON A.EMP_ID = B.EMP_ID
ORDER BY A.EMP_ID;
```

EMP_ID	EMP_LAST_NAME	EMP_FIRST_NAME	EMP_REGULAR_PAY
3217	JOHNSON	EDWARD	65000
4720	SCHULTZ	TIM	80000
6288	WILLARD	JOE	70000
7459	STEWART	BETTY	85000
9134	FRANKLIN	BRIANNA	75000

Finally let's do a join with three tables just to extend the concepts. We'll join the EMPLOYEE, EMP_PAY and EMP_PAY_HIST tables for pay date February 15 as follows:

```
SELECT A.EMP_ID,
A.EMP_LAST_NAME,
B.EMP_REGULAR_PAY,
C.EMP_PAY_AMT
FROM EMPLOYEE A
INNER JOIN EMP_PAY B ON A.EMP_ID = B.EMP_ID
INNER JOIN EMP_PAY_HIST C ON B.EMP_ID = C.EMP_ID
WHERE C.EMP_PAY_DATE = '2017-02-15';
```

EMP_ID	EMP_LAST_NAME	EMP_REGULAR_PAY	EMP_PAY_AMT
9134	FRANKLIN	75000	3125
7459	STEWART	85000	3541.67
4720	SCHULTZ	80000	3333.33
3217	JOHNSON	65000	2708.33
6288	WILLARD	70000	2916.67

Outer Joins

Now let's move on to outer joins. There are three types of outer joins. A left outer join includes matching rows from both tables plus any rows from the first table (the LEFT table) that were not matched to the other table but otherwise satisfied the WHERE condition. A right outer join includes matching rows from both tables plus any rows from the second (the RIGHT) table that were not matched to the first table, but that otherwise satisfied the WHERE condition. A full outer join includes matching rows from both tables, plus those in either table that were not matched but which otherwise satisfied the WHERE condition. We'll look at examples of all three types of outer joins.

Left Outer Join

Let's try a left outer join to include matching rows from the EMPLOYEE and EMP_PAY tables, plus any rows in the EMPLOYEE table that might not be in the EMP_PAY table. In this case we are not using a WHERE clause because the table is very small and we want to see all the results. But keep in mind that we could use a WHERE clause.

```
SELECT A.EMP_ID,
A.EMP_LAST_NAME,
A.EMP_FIRST_NAME,
B.EMP_REGULAR_PAY
FROM EMPLOYEE A
LEFT OUTER JOIN
EMP_PAY B
ON A.EMP_ID = B.EMP_ID
ORDER BY A.EMP_ID;
```

EMP_ID	EMP_LAST_NAME	EMP_FIRST_NAME	EMP_REGULAR_PAY
1122	JENKINS	DEBORAH	null
3217	JOHNSON	EDWARD	65000
3333	FORD	JAMES	null
4720	SCHULTZ	TIM	80000
6288	WILLARD	JOE	70000
7459	STEWART	BETTY	85000
7777	HARRIS	ELISA	null
9134	FRANKLIN	BRIANNA	75000

As you can see, we've included three employees who have not been assigned an annual salary yet. Deborah Jenkins, James Ford and Elisa Harris have NULL as their regular pay. The LEFT JOIN says we want all records in the first (left) table that satisfy the query even if there is no matching record in the other (right) table. That's why the query results included the three unmatched records.

Let's do another left join, and this time we'll join the EMPLOYEE table with the EMP_PAY_CHECK table. Like before, we want all records from EMPLOYEE and EMP_PAY_CHECK that match on EMP_ID, plus any EMPLOYEE records that could not be matched to EMP_PAY_CHECK.

```
SELECT A.EMP_ID,
A.EMP_LAST_NAME,
A.EMP_FIRST_NAME,
B.EMP_SEMIMTH_PAY
FROM EMPLOYEE A
LEFT OUTER JOIN
EMP_PAY_CHECK B
ON A.EMP_ID = B.EMP_ID
ORDER BY A.EMP_ID;
```

EMP_ID	EMP_LAST_NAME	EMP_FIRST_NAME	EMP_SEMIMTH_PAY
1122	JENKINS	DEBORAH	null
3217	JOHNSON	EDWARD	2708.33
3333	FORD	JAMES	null
4720	SCHULTZ	TIM	3333.33
6288	WILLARD	JOE	2916.67
7459	STEWART	BETTY	3541.67
7777	HARRIS	ELISA	null
9134	FRANKLIN	BRIANNA	3125

Again we find that three records in the EMPLOYEE table have no matching EMP_PAY_CHECK records. From a business standpoint that could be a problem unless the three are new hires who have not received their first pay check. We'll comment more on this condition shortly.

Right Outer Join

Meanwhile, now let us turn it around and do a right join. In this case we want all matching records in the EMPLOYEE and EMP_PAY_CHECK records plus any records in the EMP_PAY_CHECK tables that were not matched to the EMPLOYEE table. We can also add a WHERE condition such that the EMP_SEMIMTH_PAY column has to be populated (cannot be NULL). Let's do that.

```
SELECT B.EMP_ID,
A.EMP_LAST_NAME,
A.EMP_FIRST_NAME,
B.EMP_SEMIMTH_PAY
FROM EMPLOYEE A
RIGHT OUTER JOIN
EMP_PAY_CHECK B
ON A.EMP_ID = B.EMP_ID
WHERE EMP_SEMIMTH_PAY IS NOT NULL;
```

EMP_ID	EMP_LAST_NAME	EMP_FIRST_NAME	EMP_SEMIMTH_PAY
9134	FRANKLIN	BRIANNA	3125
7033	null	null	3208
4720	SCHULTZ	TIM	3333.33

```
7459      STEWART        BETTY            3541.67
3217      JOHNSON        EDWARD           2708.33
6288      WILLARD        JOE              2916.67
```

Now we have a case where there is a record in the EMP_PAY_CHECK table for employee 7033, but that same employee number is NOT in the EMPLOYEE table. That is something to research to find out why this condition exists.

But let's pause for a moment. You may be thinking that this is not a realistic example because any employee getting a paycheck would also have to be in the EMPLOYEE table, so this mismatch condition would never happen. I chose this example for a few reasons. One reason is to point out the importance of referential data integrity. The reason the above exception is even possible is because we haven't defined a referential relationship between these two tables (we covered referential constraints in chapter two). For now, just know that these things can and do happen when a system has not been designed with tight referential constraints in place.

A second reason I chose this example is to highlight outer joins as a useful tool in tracking down data discrepancies between tables (subqueries are another useful tool). Keep this example in mind when you are called on by your boss or your client to troubleshoot a data mismatch problem in a high pressure, time sensitive situation. You need all the tools you can get.

The third reason for choosing this example is that it very clearly demonstrates what a right join is – it includes all records from both tables that satisfy the join condition, plus any records in the "right" table that otherwise meet the WHERE condition (in this case that the EMP_SEMIMTH_PAY is populated).

Full Outer Join
Finally, let's do a full outer join to include both matched and unmatched records from both tables that meet the where condition. This will expose all the discrepancies we already uncovered with a single query.

```
SELECT A.EMP_ID,
A.EMP_LAST_NAME,
B.EMP_SEMIMTH_PAY
FROM EMPLOYEE A
FULL OUTER JOIN
EMP_PAY_CHECK B
ON A.EMP_ID = B.EMP_ID
ORDER BY A.EMP_ID;
```

EMP_ID	EMP_LAST_NAME	EMP_SEMIMTH_PAY
null	null	3208
1122	JENKINS	null
3217	JOHNSON	2708.33
3333	FORD	null
4720	SCHULTZ	3333.33
6288	WILLARD	2916.67
7459	STEWART	3541.67
7777	HARRIS	null
9134	FRANKLIN	3125

So with the FULL OUTER join we have identified the missing EMPLOYEE record, as well as the three EMP_PAY_CHECK records that are missing. Again these examples are intended both to explain the difference between the join types, and also to lend support to troubleshooting efforts where data integrity is involved.

One final comment. The outer join examples we've given so far point to potential issues with the data, and these joins are in fact helpful in diagnosing such problems. But there many cases where an entry in one table does not necessarily imply an entry in another.

For example, suppose we have an EMP_SPOUSE table that exists to administer company benefits. A person who is single has no spouse and presumably does not have an entry in the EMP_SPOUSE table. When querying for all persons covered by company benefits, an inner join between EMPLOYEE and EMP_SPOUSE would incorrectly exclude any employee who doesn't have a spouse. So you'd need a LEFT JOIN using EMPLOYEE and EMP_SPOUSE to return all insured employees plus their spouses. What I am saying is: your data model will govern what type of join is needed, so be very familiar with it.

UNION and INTERSECT
Another way to combine the results from two or more tables (or in some complex cases, to combine different result sets from a single table) is to use the UNION and INTERSECT statements. In some cases this can be preferable to doing a join.

Union
The UNION predicate combines the result sets from multiple SELECT queries. To understand how this might be useful, let's look at three examples. First, let's say we have two companies that have merged to form a third company. We have two tables EMP_COMPA and EMP_COMPB that we have structured with an EMP_ID, EMP_LAST_NAME and EMP_FIRST_NAME. We are going to structure a third table EMPLOYEE_NEW which will combine all the employees from both companies, and it will auto-generate new employee ids.

The DDL for the new table looks like this:

```
CREATE TABLE EMPLOYEE_NEW(
EMP_ID INT GENERATED ALWAYS AS IDENTITY,
EMP_OLD_ID INTEGER,
EMP_LAST_NAME VARCHAR(30) NOT NULL,
EMP_FIRST_NAME VARCHAR(20) NOT NULL);
```

Now we can load the table using a UNION as follows:

```
INSERT INTO
EMPLOYEE_NEW

SELECT EMP_ID,
EMP_LAST_NAME,
EMP_FIRST_NAME
FROM DBHR.EMP_COMPA
UNION
SELECT EMP_ID,
EMP_LAST_NAME,
EMP_FIRST_NAME
FROM DBHR.EMP_COMPB;
```

This will load the new table with data from both the old tables, and the new employee numbers will be auto-generated. Notice also we also keep the old employee numbers for cross reference if needed.

When using a UNION, the number of columns and data types must be the same for each SELECT statement. But the column names need not be the same. The UNION operation looks at the columns in the queries by position, not by name.

Let's look at two other examples of UNION actions. First, recall that earlier we used a full outer join to return all employee ids, including those that exist in one table but not the other.

```
SELECT A.EMP_ID,
B.EMP_ID,
A.EMP_LAST_NAME,
B.EMP_SEMIMTH_PAY
FROM EMPLOYEE A
FULL OUTER JOIN
EMP_PAY_CHECK B
ON A.EMP_ID = B.EMP_ID;
```

If we just needed a unique list of employee id numbers from the EMPLOYEE and EMP_PAY_CHECK tables, we could use a UNION:

```
SELECT EMP_ID
FROM EMPLOYEE
UNION
SELECT EMP_ID
FROM EMP_PAY_CHECK;

EMP_ID
1122
3217
3333
4720
6288
7033
7459
7777
9134
```

If you are wondering why we didn't get duplicate employee numbers in our list, it is because the UNION statement automatically eliminates duplicates. If for some reason you need to retain the duplicates, you would need to specify UNION ALL.

One final example will show how handy the UNION predicate is. Suppose that you want to query the EMPLOYEE table to get a list of all employee names for an upcoming company party. But you also have a contractor who (by business rules) cannot be in the EMPLOYEE table. You still want to include the contractor's name in the result set for whom to invite to the party. Let's say you want to identify the contractor with a pseudo employee-id of 9999, and the contractor's name is Janet Ko.

You could code the query as follows.

```
SELECT EMP_ID,
EMP_LAST_NAME,
EMP_FIRST_NAME
FROM EMPLOYEE
UNION
SELECT 9999,
'KO',
'JANET'
ORDER BY 1;

EMP_ID      EMP_LAST_NAME      EMP_FIRST_NAME
1122        JENKINS            DEBORAH
3217        JOHNSON            EDWARD
3333        FORD               JAMES
```

4720	SCHULTZ	TIM
6288	WILLARD	JOE
7459	STEWART	BETTY
7777	HARRIS	ELISA
9134	FRANKLIN	BRIANNA
9999	KO	JANET

Now you have listed all the employees plus your contractor friend Janet on your query results. Notice that we did not include a dummy table such as DUAL. This is because PostgreSQL neither has nor requires a dummy table for this type of query.

The UNION predicate is a useful technique when you have a "mostly" table driven system that also has some exceptions to the business rules. Sometimes a system has one-off situations that simply don't justify full blown changes to the system design. UNION can help in these cases.

Intersect

The INTERSECT predicate returns a combined result set that consists of all of the rows existing in both result sets. In one of the earlier UNION examples, we wanted all employee ids as long as they existed in either the EMPLOYEE table or the EMP_PAY_CHECK table.

```
SELECT EMP_ID
FROM EMPLOYEE
UNION
SELECT EMP_ID
FROM EMP_PAY_CHECK;
```

EMP_ID
1122
3217
3333
4720

6288
7033
7459
7777
9134

Now let's say we only want a list of employee ids that appear in both tables. The INTERSECT will accomplish that for us and we only need to change that one word in the query:

```
SELECT EMP_ID
FROM EMPLOYEE
INTERSECT
SELECT EMP_ID
FROM EMP_PAY_CHECK;

EMP_ID
119
7459
9134
4720
3217
6288
```

Common Table Expression

A common table expression is a result set that you can create and then reference in a query as though it were a table. It sometimes makes coding easier. For example, suppose we need to work with an aggregated total pay for each employee. Recall that our table named EMP_PAY_HIST includes these fields:

```
(EMP_ID INTEGER NOT NULL,
EMP_PAY_DATE DATE NOT NULL,
EMP_PAY_AMT DECIMAL (8,2) NOT NULL);
```

Assume further that we have created the following SQL that includes aggregated totals for the employees' pay. And we want to join this aggregated total data with the EMPLOYEE table to produce a final result set. Here's our SQL:

```
WITH EMP_PAY_SUM (EMP_ID, EMP_PAY_TOTAL) AS
(SELECT EMP_ID,
SUM(EMP_PAY_AMT)
AS EMP_PAY_TOTAL
FROM EMP_PAY_HIST
GROUP BY EMP_ID)

SELECT B.EMP_ID,
A.EMP_LAST_NAME,
A.EMP_FIRST_NAME,
B.EMP_PAY_TOTAL
FROM EMPLOYEE A
INNER JOIN
EMP_PAY_SUM B
ON A.EMP_ID = B.EMP_ID;
```

What we've done is to create a temporary result set named EMP_PAY_SUM that can be queried by SQL as if it were a table. This helps break down the data requirement into two pieces, one of which summarizes the pay data and the other of which adds columns from other tables to create a joined result set.

The above example may not seem like much because you could have as easily combined the two queries into one. But as your data stores get more numerous, and your queries and joins grow more complex, you may find that common table expressions can simplify queries both for you and for the developer that follows you.

Here's the result of our common table expression and the query against it.

```
WITH EMP_PAY_SUM (EMP_ID, EMP_PAY_TOTAL) AS
(SELECT EMP_ID,
SUM(EMP_PAY_AMT)
AS EMP_PAY_TOTAL
FROM EMP_PAY_HIST
GROUP BY EMP_ID)

SELECT B.EMP_ID,
A.EMP_LAST_NAME,
A.EMP_FIRST_NAME,
B.EMP_PAY_TOTAL
FROM EMPLOYEE A
INNER JOIN
EMP_PAY_SUM B
ON A.EMP_ID = B.EMP_ID
ORDER BY A.EMP_ID;
```

EMP_ID	EMP_LAST_NAME	EMP_FIRST_NAME	EMP_PAY_TOTAL
9134	FRANKLIN	BRIANNA	12500
7459	STEWART	BETTY	14166.68
4720	SCHULTZ	TIM	13333.32
3217	JOHNSON	EDWARD	10833.32
6288	WILLARD	JOE	11666.68

This concludes our discussion of the SELECT statement.

Special Registers
Special registers allow you to access detailed information about the PostgreSQL instance settings as well as certain session information. CURRENT_DATE is an example of a special register that is often used in programming (see example below). The following are SQL examples of some commonly used special registers. I suggest that you focus on these.

CURRENT_DATE

CURRENT_DATE specifies a date that is based on a reading of the time-of-day clock when the SQL statement is executed at the current server. This is often used in application programs to establish the processing date.

```
SELECT CURRENT_DATE;

Current_Date
2017-06-25
```

CURRENT_TIME

The CURRENT_TIME special register specifies a time that is based on a reading of the time-of-day clock when the SQL statement is executed at the current server.

```
SELECT CURRENT_TIME;

Current_Time(0)
15:58:07-04:00
```

CURRENT_TIMESTAMP

The CURRENT_TIMESTAMP special register specifies a timestamp based on the time-of-day clock at the current server.

```
SELECT CURRENT_TIMESTAMP;

Current_TimeStamp(6)
2017-06-25 15:58:56.380000-04:00
```

Built-In Functions

Built-in functions can be used in SQL statements to return a result based on an argument. These functions are great productivity tools because they can replace custom coded functionality in an application program. Whether your role is application developer, DBA or business services professional, the PostgreSQL built-in functions can save you a great deal of time and effort if you know what they are and how to use them.

There are two types of built-in functions:

1. Aggregate

2. Scalar

We'll look at examples of each of these types.

Aggregate Functions

An aggregate function receives a set of values for each argument (such as the values of a column) and returns a single-value result for the set of input values. These are especially useful in data analytics. Here are some examples of commonly used aggregate functions.

AVERAGE

The average function returns the average of a set of numbers. Using our EMP_PAY table, you could get the average REGULAR_PAY for your employees like this:

```
SELECT AVG(EMP_REGULAR_PAY)
FROM EMP_PAY;

AVG
75000
```

COUNT

The COUNT function returns the number of rows or values in a set of rows or values. Suppose you want to know how many employees you have. You could use this SQL to find out:

```
SELECT COUNT(*) AS EMP_CNT
FROM EMPLOYEE;

EMP_CNT
9
```

MAX

The MAX function returns the maximum value in a set of values.

MIN

The MIN function returns the minimum value in a set of values. In the next two examples, we use the MAX and MIN functions to determine the highest and lowest paid employees:

```
SELECT MAX(EMP_REGULAR_PAY)
FROM EMP_PAY;

EMP_REGULAR_PAY
85000
```

Now if we want to know both the maximum salary and the employee who earns it, it is a bit more complex, but not much. We just need to add a subquery.

```
SELECT EMP_ID, EMP_REGULAR_PAY
FROM EMP_PAY
WHERE EMP_REGULAR_PAY =
(SELECT MAX(EMP_REGULAR_PAY) FROM EMP_PAY);


EMP_ID    EMP_REGULAR_PAY
7459        85000
```

Similarly, we can find the minimum using the MIN function.

```
SELECT MIN(EMP_REGULAR_PAY)
FROM EMP_PAY;


EMP_REGULAR_PAY
65000

SELECT EMP_ID, EMP_REGULAR_PAY
FROM EMP_PAY
WHERE EMP_REGULAR_PAY =
(SELECT MIN(EMP_REGULAR_PAY) FROM EMP_PAY);


EMP_ID EMP_REGULAR_PAY
3217    65000
```

SUM

The SUM function returns the sum of a set of numbers. Suppose you need to know what your base payroll will be for the year. You could find out with this SQL:

```
SELECT SUM(EMP_REGULAR_PAY) AS EMP_REGULAR_PAY
FROM EMP_PAY;


EMP_REGULAR_PAY
375000
```

Scalar Functions

A scalar function can be used wherever an expression can be used. It is often used to calculate a value or to influence the result of a query. Again we'll provide some examples.

COALESCE

The COALESCE function returns the value of the first non-null expression. It is normally used to assign some alternate value when a NULL value is encountered that would otherwise cause an entire record containing the NULL to be excluded from the results. For example, consider the EMP_PAY table with data as follows:

```
SELECT * FROM EMP_PAY;

EMP_ID          EMP_REGULAR_PAY         EMP_BONUS_PAY
9134            75000                   2500
7459            85000                   4000
4720            80000                   2500
3217            65000                   5500
6288            70000                   2000
```

To demonstrate how COALESCE works, let's first change the bonus pay amount for employee 9134 to NULL.

```
UPDATE EMP_PAY
SET EMP_BONUS_PAY = NULL
WHERE EMP_ID = 9134;
```

Now our data looks like this:

```
SELECT * FROM EMP_PAY;

EMP_ID          EMP_REGULAR_PAY         EMP_BONUS_PAY
9134            75000                   null
7459            85000                   4000
4720            80000                   2500
3217            65000                   5500
6288            70000                   2000
```

Ok, here's the example. Let's find the average bonus pay in the EMP_PAY table.

```
SELECT AVG(EMP_BONUS_PAY)
AS AVERAGE_BONUS
FROM EMP_PAY;

AVERAGE_BONUS
3500
```

If we look at this result and do a bit of arithmetic, we can see there is a problem here! The problem is that the average bonus is not 3500, it is 2800 (total 14,000 bonus pay divided by five employees). The problem here is that one of the employee records has NULL in the EMP_BONUS_PAY column. Consequently this record was excluded from the calculated average because NULL is not a numeric value and therefore cannot be included in a numeric computation.

112

Assuming that you do want to include this record in your results to get the correct average, what we need is to convert the NULL to numeric value zero for purposes of the query. You can do this using the COALESCE function.

```
SELECT AVG(COALESCE(EMP_BONUS_PAY,0))
AS AVERAGE_BONUS
FROM EMP_PAY;

AVERAGE_BONUS
2800
```

The above says to calculate the average EMP_BONUS_PAY using the first non-null value of EMP_BONUS_PAY or zero. Since employee 9134 has a NULL value in the EMP_BONUS_PAY field, PostgreSQL substitutes a zero instead of the NULL. Zero is a numeric value, so this record can now be included in the computation of the average. This gives the correct average which is 2800.

Before we move on let's reset the bonus pay on our employee 9134 so that it can be used correctly for other queries later in the text book.

```
UPDATE EMP_PAY
SET EMP_BONUS_PAY = 2500.00
WHERE EMP_ID = 9134;
```

You can use COALESCE anytime you need to include a record that would otherwise be excluded due to a NULL value. Converting the NULL to an actual value will ensure the record can be included in the results.

CONCAT

The CONCAT function combines two or more strings. Suppose for example you want to list each employee's first and last names from the EMPLOYEE table. You could so it with this SQL:

```
SELECT
CONCAT(CONCAT(EMP_FIRST_NAME,' '),EMP_LAST_NAME)
AS EMP_FULL_NAME
FROM EMPLOYEE;

EMP_FULL_NAME
BRIANNA FRANKLIN
FRED TURNBULL
TIM SCHULTZ
DEBORAH JENKINS
```

```
EDWARD JOHNSON
BETTY STEWART
ELISA HARRIS
JAMES FORD
JOE WILLARD
```

DATE_PART

The DATE_PART function allows you to reference specific parts of a date such as month, day and year. Here's an example.

```
SELECT
EMP_ID,
EMP_PROMOTION_DATE,
CURRENT_DATE AS RQST_DATE
FROM EMPLOYEE
WHERE DATE_PART('MONTH', EMP_PROMOTION_DATE)
= DATE_PART('MONTH', DATE '2017-01-01')
ORDER BY EMP_ID;
```

EMP_ID	EMP_PROMOTION_DATE	RQST_DATE
3217	2017-01-01	2017-01-19
4720	2017-01-01	2017-01-19
6288	2016-01-01	2017-01-19

LOWER

The LOWER function returns a string in which all the characters to which it applies are converted to lowercase characters. Note: this function does not change any value on the table, it is only formatting the value for presentation.

```
SELECT EMP_ID, LOWER(EMP_LAST_NAME)
FROM EMPLOYEE;
```

EMP_ID	EMP_LAST_NAME
9134	franklin
4175	turnbull
4720	schultz
1122	jenkins
3217	johnson
7459	stewart
7777	harris
3333	ford
6288	willard

LEFT

The LEFT function returns a string that consists of the specified number of leftmost bytes of the specified string units. Suppose you have an application that needs the first four letters of the last name (my pharmacy does this as part of the automated prescription filling process). You could accomplish that with this SQL:

```
SELECT EMP_ID, LEFT(EMP_LAST_NAME,4) AS NAME_FIRST_4
FROM EMPLOYEE;
```

```
EMP_ID NAME_FIRST_4
9134   FRAN
4175   TURN
4720   SCHU
1122   JENK
3217   JOHN
7459   STEW
7777   HARR
3333   FORD
6288   WILL
```

SUBSTR

The SUBSTR function returns a substring of a string. Let's use the earlier example of retrieving the first four letters of the last name via the LEFT function. You could also accomplish that with this SQL:

```
SELECT EMP_ID, SUBSTR(EMP_LAST_NAME,1,4)
FROM EMPLOYEE;
```

```
EMP_ID EMP_LAST_NAME
9134   FRAN
4175   TURN
4720   SCHU
1122   JENK
3217   JOHN
7459   STEW
7777   HARR
3333   FORD
6288   WILL
```

The 1,4 means starting in position one for a length of four. Of course, you could use a different starting position.

UPPER
The UPPER function returns a string in which all the characters are converted to uppercase characters. Here is an example of actually changing the last name of each employee to upper case. First we will have to covert the uppercase EMP_LAST_NAME values to lowercase. We can do that using the LOWER function. Let's do this for a single row:

```
UPDATE EMPLOYEE
SET EMP_LAST_NAME
  = LOWER(EMP_LAST_NAME) WHERE EMP_ID = 3217;
```

We can verify that the data did in fact get changed to lower case.

```
SELECT EMP_LAST_NAME
FROM EMPLOYEE
WHERE EMP_ID = 3217;
```

EMP_LAST_NAME
johnson

Now let's use the UPPER function to have the EMP_LAST_NAME display as upper case.

```
SELECT EMP_ID, UPPER(EMP_LAST_NAME)
FROM EMPLOYEE
WHERE EMP_ID = 3217;
```

EMP_ID   **EMP_LAST_NAME**
3217   JOHNSON

Note that the SELECT query did not actually change any data on the table. We have simply reformatted the data for presentation. Now let's actually convert the data on the record back to upper case:

```
UPDATE EMPLOYEE
SET EMP_LAST_NAME = UPPER(EMP_LAST_NAME)
WHERE EMP_ID = 3217;
```

And we'll verify that it reverted back to uppercase:

```
SELECT EMP_LAST_NAME
FROM EMPLOYEE
WHERE EMP_ID = 3217;
```

EMP_LAST_NAME
JOHNSON

This concludes our basic discussion of DML. I recommend that you do the chapter execises.

Chapter Three Exercises

1. Write a query to display the last and first names of all employees in the EMPLOYEE table. Display the names in alphabetic order by EMP_LAST_NAME.

2. Write a query to change the first name of Edward Johnson (employee 3217) to Eddie.

3. Write a query to produce the number of employees in the EMPLOYEE table.

Chapter Four: PostgreSQL Application Programming

Java PostgreSQL Programming

In this section we will look at how to work with PostgreSQL using the Java programming language. Specifically we will learn how to connect to a PostgreSQL database, and how to retrieve and update data from a table.

Note: In this section we will be using the Java Oxygen Eclipse IDE. If you already have another IDE, feel free to use it. If you'd like to install Java Oxygen the link to acquire it (and the installation instructions) are in Appendix 3.

Sample Java PostgreSQL Program

To work with PostgreSQL in the Java programming language, you must:

1. Establish a Connection

2. Construct either a Statement or a PreparedStatement

3. Execute the Statement or Prepared Statement

4. Construct a ResultSet object to either read or update the query data

5. Handle any Errors

Let's start with a simple example where we will query the EMPLOYEE database for the first and last name of employee 3217. For this first example we will show creating the Java program in Eclipse Java Oxygen. For subsequent programs we will simply show the source code.

First, open Eclipse Java Oxygen and change to the Java perspective (if not already there). If you do not see the Package Explorer view, click on **Window → Show View → Package Explorer** field and click on Next.

Now click on **File → New Java Project**. Enter "employee" in the Project Name. Then click **Next**.

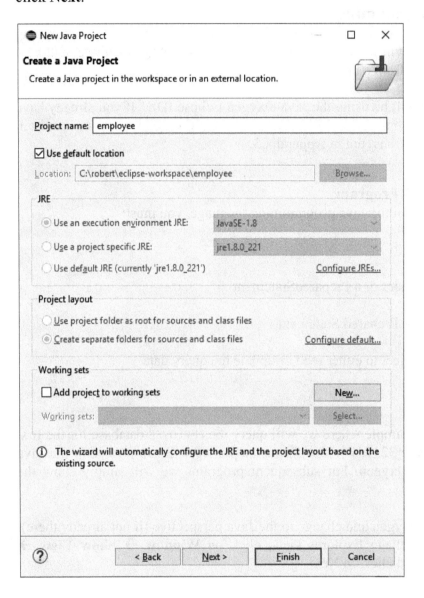

On the next panel, click on the Libraries tab. Here you must specify the PostgreSQL JDBC connection driver which is a file named **postgresql-42.2.5.jar**. You can find this file in the PostgreSQL JDBC folder under `Program Files (x86)/PostgreSQL/pgJDBC`.

If you did not install the JDBC driver when we did the original installation of PostgreSQL, you can download it from here.

https://jdbc.postgresql.org/download.html

Meanwhile, on the libraries tab, click on **Add External JARs**.

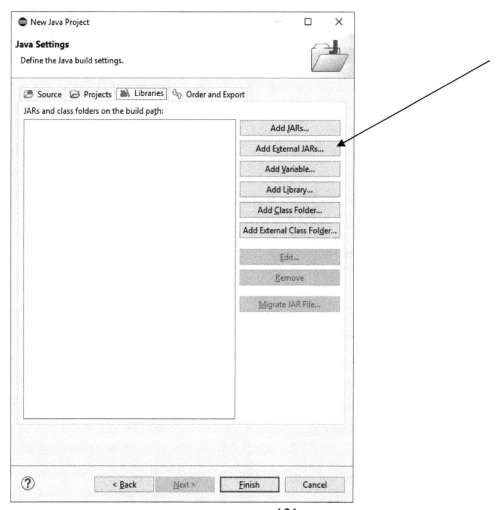

Navigate to the JDBC driver folder and select the file named **postgresql-42.2.5.jar.**
Click on **Open.**

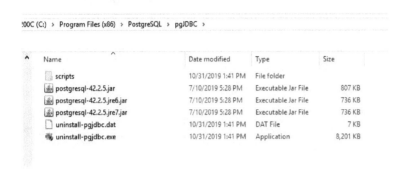

As you can see, the PostgreSQL jar file is added to the libraries. If your Java system
library was not added by default, you must do so now. Click **Add Library.**

Choose JRE System Library, then click **Next**.

The system has located JRE 1.8 on my local disk. I'll use this as my default when in Eclipse. Click **Finish**.

Verify that the JRE is added to your library list, as mine is below. Then click **Finish**.

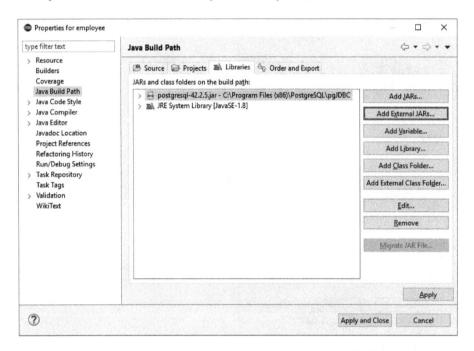

Now in the Project Explorer, select employee, right click and select **New Package**.

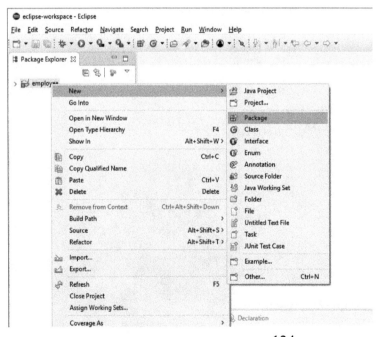

Type **employee** in the name field and then click **Finish**.

In the Package Explorer, right click on the package **employee** and select **New Class**. Let's name our class EmpInfo which you should type in the **Name** field. Also check the box to generate a stub for a main stub. Then click **Finish**.

Your structure should look like this, and your new class should appear in the right portion of the screen.

Let's first code the connection. I'm going to give you a screen shot for Eclipse and then I am going to show you the code in a listing. I think you'll find the latter easier to read.

```
*EmpInfo.java ☒
1  package employee;
2
3  import java.sql.*;
4
5  public class EmpInfo {
6
7      public static void main(String[] args) throws ClassNotFoundException {
8          Class.forName("org.postgresql.Driver");
9          System.out.println("**** Loaded the JDBC driver");
10         String url = "jdbc:postgresql:DBHR?user=postgres&password=postgres";
11         Connection con = null;
12
13         try {
14             con = DriverManager.getConnection(url);
15             System.out.println("**** Created the PostgreSQL connection");
16
17
18         } catch (SQLException e) {
19             System.out.println(e.getMessage());
20             System.out.println(e.getErrorCode());
21             e.printStackTrace();
22
23         }
24
25     }
26
27 }
28
29 |
```

And here is the code in more readable format. As you can see we set up a few variables for the connection, and we are using the getConnection method of the connection object to establish a connection. We also coded an error handler to intercept any SQL errors we encounter.

```
package employee;
import java.sql.*;
public class EmpInfo {

    public static void main(String[] args) throws ClassNotFoundException {

        Class.forName("org.postgresql.Driver");
        System.out.println("**** Loaded the JDBC driver");
        String url
            = "jdbc:postgresql:DBHR?user=postgres&password=postgres";

        Connection con = null;

        try {
            con = DriverManager.getConnection(url);
            System.out.println("**** Created the PostgreSQL connection");
```

```
        } catch (SQLException e) {
                System.out.println(e.getMessage());

                System.out.println(e.getErrorCode());

                e.printStackTrace();

        }
    }

}
```

Let's test our code by running the program. Click on the green forward arrow at the top of the screen. And then check the Console window tab for the result.

```
🖥 Console ✕
<terminated> EmpInfo [Java Application] C:\Program Files\Java\jre1.8.0_231\bin\javaw.exe (Nov 1, 2019, 3:24:28 PM)
**** Loaded the JDBC driver
**** Created the PostgreSQL connection
```

As you can see, our code execution was successful - we connected to PostgreSQL. Of course, that's just the first part of our task. Now we need some SQL to retrieve our EMPLOYEE information. To do that, we must create a String object to contain our query, a Statement object to execute the query and a ResultSet object to contain the results from the query.

Here is our current version of the program code with these additional features. Notice also that as we cycle through the result set, we are going to display the employee's last and first name in the console.

```
package employee;
import java.sql.*;

public class EmpInfo {

        public static void main(String[] args) throws ClassNotFoundException {

                Class.forName("org.postgresql.Driver");
                System.out.println("**** Loaded the JDBC driver");
                String url
                    = "jdbc:postgresql:DBHR?user=postgres&password=postgres";

                Connection con = null;
```

```
        try {
                con = DriverManager.getConnection(url);
                System.out.println("**** Created the PostgreSQL connection");

                String query = "SELECT EMP_LAST_NAME,"
                        + "EMP_FIRST_NAME "
                        + "FROM EMPLOYEE " + "WHERE EMP_ID = 3217";
                Statement stmt;
                stmt = con.createStatement();
                ResultSet rs = stmt.executeQuery(query);
                while (rs.next()) {
                        String strLastName = rs.getString(1);
                        String strFirstName = rs.getString(2);
                        System.out.println("Last name is     " + strLastName);
                        System.out.println("First name is " + strFirstName);
                }

        } catch (SQLException e) {
                System.out.println(e.getMessage());
                System.out.println(e.getErrorCode());
                e.printStackTrace();

        }
    }

}
```

Finally, let's look at the console to get the results:

```
28              } catch (SQLException e) {
29                  System.out.println(e.getMessage());
30                  System.out.println(e.getErrorCode());
31                  e.printStackTrace();
32
33              }
34
35          }
36
37  }
38
39
```

```
Console
<terminated> EmpInfo [Java Application] C:\Program Files\Java\jre1.8.0_231\bin\javaw.exe (Nov 1, 2019, 3:27:02 PM)
**** Loaded the JDBC driver
**** Created the PostgreSQL connection
Last name is     JOHNSON
First name is EDWARD
```

I've also cut and pasted the results here to make it easier to read:

```
**** Loaded the JDBC driver
**** Created the connection
Last name is JOHNSON
First name is EDWARD
```

For the rest of the Java examples, I will simply provide you with the code instead of showing the IDE. This will save some space and it is easier to read.

To review our example, what the Java code does is to:

1. Create a connection, connect to the DBHR database

2. Create a query string to read the EMPLOYEE table

3. Execute the query using a Statement object

4. Read the query results using a ResultSet object

5. Load the result set data to string variables

6. Display the data using the println method

Granted this program does not do much, but it did successfully connect to PostgreSQL and retrieved data from it. That's what we wanted to accomplish!

Java PostgreSQL INSERT Program

For the insert program, we only need to change a few things that we used in the query program. Of course we must change the SQL to an INSERT statement. Also, instead of creating a result set, we only need to execute the query with the executeUpdate method of the Statement object. Here is our listing.

```java
package employee;
import java.sql.*;

public class JAVEMP1 {

        public static void main(String[] args) throws ClassNotFoundException {
                Class.forName("org.postgresql.Driver");
                System.out.println("**** Loaded the JDBC driver");
                String url
                    = "jdbc:postgresql:DBHR?user=postgres&password=postgres";
```

```java
        Connection con = null;

        try {
                con = DriverManager.getConnection(url);

                System.out.println("**** Created the connection");

                String query = "INSERT INTO EMPLOYEE "
                        + "(EMP_ID, "
                        + "EMP_LAST_NAME, "
                        + "EMP_FIRST_NAME, "
                        + "EMP_SERVICE_YEARS, "
                        + "EMP_PROMOTION_DATE) "
                        + "VALUES (1111, "
                        + "'VEREEN', "
                        + "'CHARLES', "
                        + "12, " + "'2017-01-01') ";

                Statement stmt;
                stmt = con.createStatement();
                stmt.executeUpdate(query);
                System.out.println("Successful INSERT of employee "
                    + 1111);

        } catch (SQLException e) {
                System.out.println(e.getMessage());
                System.out.println(e.getErrorCode());
                e.printStackTrace();

        }

    }

}
```

When you run this program, you should receive this output in the console window:

```
**** Loaded the JDBC driver
**** Created the connection Successful INSERT of employee 1111
```

And we can verify the INSERT by checking the table.

```
SELECT * FROM
EMPLOYEE
WHERE EMP_ID = 1111;
```

EMP_ID	EMP_LAST_NAME	EMP_FIRST_NAME	EMP_SERVICE_YEARS	EMP_PROMOTION_DATE
1111	VEREEN	CHARLES	12	2017-01-01

Note: you could have also omitted the target columns and simply coded the INSERT statement as follows:

```
String query = "INSERT INTO EMPLOYEE "
+ "VALUES (1111, "
+ "'VEREEN', "
+ "'CHARLES', "
+ "12, "
+ "'01/01/2017') " ;
```

Before we move on, let's check the error handling code. Let's try to add the same record again, which should result in an SQL Exception. And in fact we do trap an exception which is a 2801 error code which means a record already exists with the same key. Here is the result shown in the console:

```
**** Loaded the JDBC driver
**** Created the connection
ERROR: duplicate key value violates unique constraint "employee_pkey"
   Detail: Key (emp_id)=(1111) already exists.
```

Good, this is what we expected. Now let's move on to an insert with parameter markers.

Java PostgreSQL INSERT Program with Parameter Markers
When processing multiple records you can use parameter markers with the VALUES clause. A parameter marker is a character (typically the question mark character "?") that serves as a placeholder for an unknown value that will be passed to the SQL using the various set methods of the statement object.

Let's add another record and this time we'll build the SQL using parameter markers. We'll supply the values at run time using the set methods of our Statement object (such as setInt, setString, etc).

```
package employee;
import java.text.*;
import java.sql.*;

public class JAVEMP1A {
```

```java
    public static void main(String[] args) throws ClassNotFoundException,
ParseException {
        Class.forName("org.postgresql.Driver");
        System.out.println("**** Loaded the JDBC driver");
        String url
            = "jdbc:postgresql:DBHR?user=postgres&password=postgres";

        Connection con = null;

        try {

                con = DriverManager.getConnection(url);
                System.out.println("**** Created the connection");

                String query = "INSERT INTO EMPLOYEE "
                    + "VALUES (?, " + "?, " + "?, " + "?, " + "?) ";

                PreparedStatement stmt;
                stmt = con.prepareStatement(query);

                stmt.setInt(1, 1112);
                stmt.setString(2, "YATES");
                stmt.setString(3, "JANENE");
                stmt.setInt(4, 7);

                DateFormat df = new SimpleDateFormat("yyyy-MM-dd");
                java.sql.Date datProm
                    = new java.sql.Date(df.parse("2015-01-01").getTime());
                stmt.setDate(5, datProm);

                stmt.executeUpdate();

                System.out.println("Successful INSERT of employee "
                    + 1112);

        }

        catch (SQLException e) {

                System.out.println(e.getMessage());
                System.out.println(e.getErrorCode());
                e.printStackTrace();

        }

    }
```

```
}
```

And again we successfully inserted an employee record:

```
**** Loaded the JDBC driver
**** Created the connection Successful INSERT of employee 1112
```

The PreparedStatement object is especially useful when you have multiple records to process and you want to use the same SQL statement and just reset the parameter values. In some respects this works like host variables in embedded SQL programs.

Java PostgreSQL UPDATE Program

Now let's look at a process we performed earlier for changing lowercase characters in the surname to upper case.

```
UPDATE EMPLOYEE
SET EMP_LAST_NAME = LOWER(EMP_LAST_NAME)
WHERE EMP_LAST_NAME IN ('JOHNSON', 'STEWART', 'FRANKLIN');

SELECT EMP_LAST_NAME FROM EMPLOYEE
WHERE EMP_LAST_NAME <> UPPER(EMP_LAST_NAME);


EMP_LAST_NAME
franklin
stewart
johnson
```

Now here is our Java program to change lower case to uppercase. We're creating a ResultSet object that contains the records we need to modify. We walk through the result set and move the surname to a string object. We modify the string using the Java toUpperCase() string function. Then we use the ResultSet updateString() method to replace the EMP_LAST_NAME column of the result set, and then we use updateRow() to apply the modified record to the table. Finally, we finalize our update records using the commit() method of the Connection object.

```
package employee;
import java.sql.*;

public class JAVEMP2 {

        public static void main(String[] args) throws ClassNotFoundException {
                Class.forName("org.postgresql.Driver");
```

```java
        System.out.println("**** Loaded the JDBC driver");
        String url
            = "jdbc:postgresql:DBHR?user=postgres&password=postgres";

        Connection con = null;
        try {
                con = DriverManager.getConnection(url);
                System.out.println("**** Created the connection");
                String query = "SELECT EMP_ID, EMP_LAST_NAME "
                + "FROM EMPLOYEE "
                + "WHERE EMP_LAST_NAME <> UPPER(EMP_LAST_NAME)";

                Integer intEmpNo;
                String strLastName;
                Statement stmt;
                stmt
                    = con.createStatement(ResultSet.TYPE_SCROLL_SENSITIVE,
                ResultSet.CONCUR_UPDATABLE,
                ResultSet.HOLD_CURSORS_OVER_COMMIT);
                ResultSet rs = stmt.executeQuery(query);

                while (rs.next()) {
                        intEmpNo = rs.getInt(1);
                        strLastName = rs.getString(2);
                        System.out.println("Employee " + intEmpNo
                        + " BEFORE Last name is: " + strLastName);
                        strLastName = strLastName.toUpperCase();
                        rs.updateString(2, strLastName);
                        rs.updateRow();
                        System.out.println("Employee " + intEmpNo
                        + " AFTER  Last name is: " + strLastName);
                }


        } catch (SQLException e) {
                System.out.println(e.getMessage());
                System.out.println(e.getErrorCode());
                e.printStackTrace();

        }
    }
}
```

And this is our output:

```
**** Loaded the JDBC driver
```

```
**** Created the connection
Employee 3217 BEFORE Last name is: johnson
Employee 3217 AFTER   Last name is: JOHNSON
Employee 7459 BEFORE Last name is: stewart
Employee 7459 AFTER   Last name is: STEWART
Employee 9134 BEFORE Last name is: franklin
Employee 9134 AFTER   Last name is: FRANKLIN
```

Finally, let's verify that the data was set back to upper case.

```
SELECT EMP_LAST_NAME FROM EMPLOYEE
WHERE EMP_LAST_NAME IN ('JOHNSON', 'STEWART', 'FRANKLIN');

EMP_LAST_NAME
FRANKLIN
STEWART
JOHNSON
```

The method of using a positioned update based on a ResultSet is something you will use often, particularly when you do not know your result set content beforehand, and anytime you need to examine the content of the record before you perform the update or delete action.

I'll leave the delete and merge statements for chapter exercises. I think you get the general idea of how to build SQL statements and run them in Java using the Connection object, the Statement (or PreparedStatement) object, and the ResultSet object.

.NET PostgreSQL Programming

In this section we will look at how to work with PostgreSQL using the c# .NET programming language. Specifically we will learn how to connect to a PostgreSQL database, and how to retrieve and update data from a table.

Sample .NET PostgreSQL Program

Basic RDMS objects and methods

To work with PostgreSQL using .NET is similar to using Java. The object names and methods are somewhat different though.

1. Establish a Connection

2. Construct a command

3. Construct a DataReader object if you are reading data (otherwise you can use the command object to execute a non-query action).

4. Construct a DataAdaptor object and a DataSet object if you are updating data.

5. Handle any Errors.

There are three types of PostgreSQL data providers using .NET:

1. PostgreSQL .NET Data Provider

2. OleDB .NET Data Provider

3. ODBC .NET Data Provider

We'll mostly use the PostgreSQL .NET data provider, but for our example program we'll also show a version using ODBC. Let's start with the same example we used with Java where we query the EMPLOYEE database for the first and last name of an employee.

For this first example we will show creating the .NET c# program in Visual Studio 2017 Community edition. For subsequent programs we will simply display the c# source code as I think it is easier for you to read.

Begin by opening Visual Studio 2017. You will see the Getting Started screen. Select **File → New → Project.**

Now select the type of project. In our case we will select a Visual C# Console App (.NET framework). Type the name of your first project into the Name field. In my case I will name it NETEMP0. Then click **OK**.

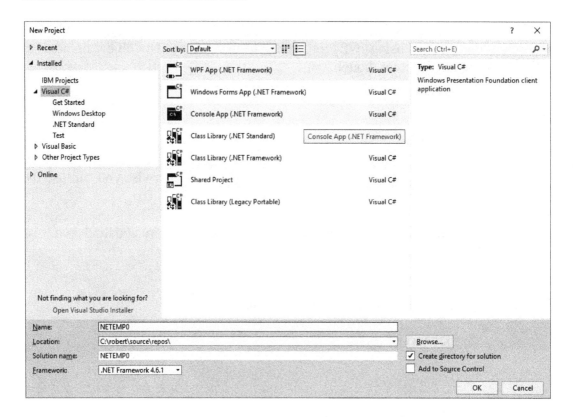

Now you will see this window with a program framework already filled in. First, change the program name in the solution explorer by right clicking it and selecting rename – let's use the name NETEMP0.

When prompted to rename references to the program to NETEMP0, click on **Yes**.

You'll notice the various "Using" entries at the beginning of the program. These are basically package names. We want to use the PostgreSQL .NET data provider, so we must include this line of code (make sure the word "using" is in lower case). :

```
using Npgsql;
```

However, when we add it, Visual Studio tells us the namespace is unknown.

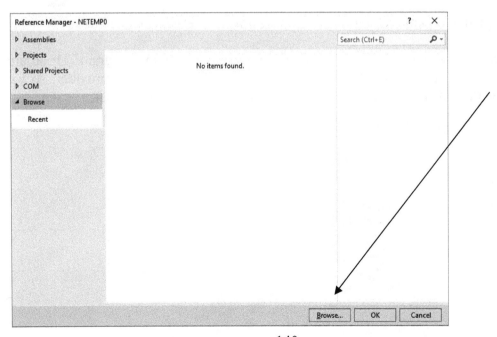

```
:gram.cs*  ⇄ X
NETEMP0                                                   ▾ | ⭐ NETEMP0.NETEMP0
    1  ⊟using System;
    2   using System.Collections.Generic;
    3   using System.Linq;
    4   using System.Text;
    5   using System.Threading.Tasks;
    6   using Npgsql;
    7      ┌─────────────────────────────────────────────────────────────────────────────────────────┐
    8  ⊟namespace │ Using directive is unnecessary.                                                    │
    9   {          │                                                                                   │
   10  ⊟    class  │ The type or namespace name 'Npgsql' could not be found (are you missing a using directive or an assembly reference?) │
   11        {     │                                                                                   │
   12  ⊟        static void Main(string[] args)   Show potential fixes (Alt+Enter or Ctrl+.)           │
   13        {      └─────────────────────────────────────────────────────────────────────────────────┘
   14
   15            NpgsqlConnection conn = null;
   16            try
   17            {
   18                conn = new NpgsqlConnection("Server=127.0.0.1; Port=5432; User ID=postgres; password=postgres; Database=DBHR");
   19                conn.Open();
   20                Console.WriteLine("Successful PostgreSQL connection!");
   21
   22            }
   23
   24            catch (Exception e)
   25            {
   26                Console.WriteLine(e.Message);
   27            }
   28
   29            finally
   30            {
   31                conn.Close();
   32            }
   33
   34          }
   35      }
   36
   37  }
   38
```

To fix this, we must add a reference to the PostgreSQL .NET DLL file in your PostgreSQL installation directory. Click on **Project → Add Reference**. When the Reference Manager window opens, click on Browse.

Navigate to your PostgreSQL install directory. On my PC this is:

```
C:\Program Files(x86)\PostgreSQL\Npgsql
```

Click on the **Npgsql.dll** file and then click **Add**.

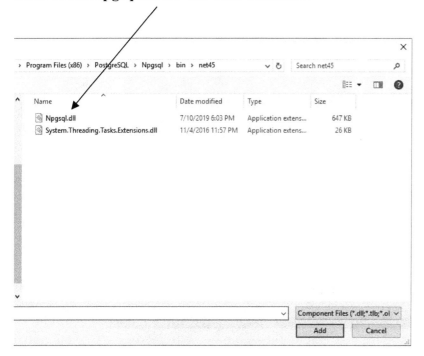

You will now see that the DLL has been added to the project. Click OK.

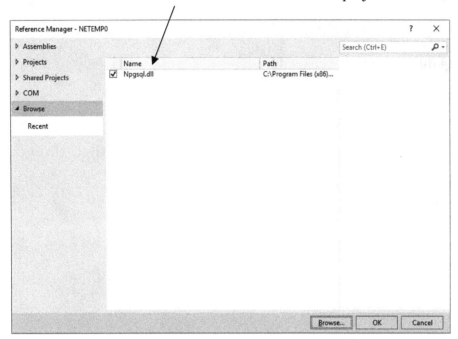

Also, you will see there is no longer an error in the program listing.

```
Program.cs* ≠ ×
C# NETEMP0                                                    ▾ ⁑ NETEMP0.NETEMP0
     1    ⊟using System;
     2     using System.Collections.Generic;
     3     using System.Linq;
     4     using System.Text;
     5     using System.Threading.Tasks;
     6     using Npgsql;
     7
     8    ⊟namespace NETEMP0
     9     {
    10    ⊟    class NETEMP0
    11         {
    12    ⊟        static void Main(string[] args)
    13             {
    14
    15                 NpgsqlConnection conn = null;
    16    ⊟            try
    17                 {
    18                     conn = new NpgsqlConnection("Server=127.0.0.1; Port=5432; User ID=postgres; password=postgres; Database=DBHR");
    19                     conn.Open();
    20                     Console.WriteLine("Successful PostgreSQL connection!");
    21
    22                 }
    23
    24                 catch (Exception e)
    25                 {
    26                     Console.WriteLine(e.Message);
    27                 }
    28
    29                 finally
    30                 {
    31                     conn.Close();
    32                 }
    33
    34             }
    35         }
    36
    37    └}
    38
```

We need to make one more configuration change to the project, which is to change the output type from console application to windows application. If we don't do that, our output will appear in a black console window and disappear after a couple of seconds. We want our output to appear in the Output window in the IDE, and to persist so that we can look at it!

So click on **Project → NETEMP0** Properties. Then change the Output Type from Console Application to Windows Application, and then close this window.

Now let's add the appropriate c# code to create our connection, command and data reader objects. Also we will add code to run the query and display the last and first name of the employee with employee id 3217.

```csharp
Program.cs*
NETEMP0                                                               NETEMP0.NETEMP0
4     using System.Text;
5     using System.Threading.Tasks;
6     using Npgsql;
7
8     namespace NETEMP0
9     {
10        class NETEMP0
11        {
12            static void Main(string[] args)
13            {
14
15                NpgsqlConnection conn = null;
16                NpgsqlCommand cmd = null;
17                NpgsqlDataReader rdr = null;
18                bool rows = false;
19                int cols = 0;
20
21                try
22                {
23                    conn = new NpgsqlConnection("Server=127.0.0.1; Port=5432; User ID=postgres; password=postgres; Database=DBHR");
24                    conn.Open();
25                    Console.WriteLine("Successful PostgreSQL connection!");
26
27                    cmd = conn.CreateCommand();
28                    cmd.CommandText
29                        = "SELECT EMP_LAST_NAME,"
30                        + "EMP_FIRST_NAME "
31                        + "FROM EMPLOYEE "
32                        + "WHERE EMP_ID = 3217";
33
34                    rdr = cmd.ExecuteReader();
35                    Console.WriteLine("\nExecute: " + cmd.CommandText);
36
37                    cols = rdr.FieldCount;
38                    rows = rdr.HasRows;
39
40                    while (rdr.Read() == true)
41                    {
42                        Console.WriteLine("Last name is : " + rdr.GetString(0));
43                        Console.WriteLine("First name is : " + rdr.GetString(1));
44                    }
45
```

To more easily read the code (and since we can't get it all in one window anyway), I'll give you the entire listing here.

Note: In some cases for readability in this book I had to wrap a line of code, such as for the connection assignment statement. Doing this in the IDE will give you an error, so you'll actually need to put the entire statement on one line like:

```
conn = new NpgsqlConnection("Server=127.0.0.1; Port=5432; User ID=postgres; password=postgres; Database=DBHR");
```

Ok, here's the listing.

```csharp
using System;
using System.Collections.Generic;
using System.Linq;
using System.Text;
using System.Threading.Tasks;
using Npgsql;

namespace NETEMP0
{
    class NETEMP0
    {
        static void Main(string[] args)
        {

            NpgsqlConnection conn = null;
            NpgsqlCommand cmd = null;
            NpgsqlDataReader rdr = null;
            bool rows = false;
            int cols = 0;

            try
            {
                conn = new NpgsqlConnection("Server=127.0.0.1; Port=5432;
                    User ID=postgres; password=postgres; Database=DBHR");
                conn.Open();
                Console.WriteLine("Successful PostgreSQL connection!");

                cmd = conn.CreateCommand();
                cmd.CommandText
                    = "SELECT EMP_LAST_NAME,"
                        + "EMP_FIRST_NAME "
                        + "FROM EMPLOYEE "
                        + "WHERE EMP_ID = 3217";

                rdr = cmd.ExecuteReader();
                Console.WriteLine("\nExecute: " + cmd.CommandText);

                cols = rdr.FieldCount;
```

144

```
        rows = rdr.HasRows;

        while (rdr.Read() == true)
        {
            Console.WriteLine("Last name is : " + rdr.GetString(0));
            Console.WriteLine("First name is : " + rdr.GetString(1));
        }

    }

    catch (Exception e)
    {
        Console.WriteLine(e.Message);
    }

    finally
    {
        Console.WriteLine("Returned Rows? " + rows);
        conn.Close();
    }

        }
    }

}
```

Now we can execute this program by clicking on the Start button (the forward green arrow at the top of the window which also reads "Start". You will see the result of the program execution in the Output window at the bottom:

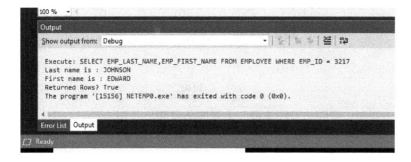

Congratulations, you have just run a .NET program to access and return data from a PostgreSQL database!

Here's the output in easier-to-read format:

```
Execute: SELECT EMP_LAST_NAME,EMP_FIRST_NAME FROM EMPLOYEE WHERE EMP_ID = 3217

Last name is : JOHNSON
First name is : EDWARD
Returned Rows? True
```

Sample .NET ODBC Program

The ODBC interface is a bit different in terms of the objects, but more or less the same in terms of the code. For the most part you'll see those objects previously prefixed "Td" replaced here with objects prefixed with "ODBC".

Note that you must have registered the PostgreSQL database you are reading as an ODBC data source (typically via Control Panel Administrative Tools ODBC Data Sources). Otherwise you cannot use the ODBC data provider.

Here is my ODBC entry:

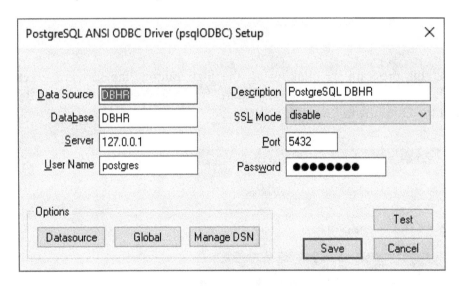

And here is the program code:

```
using System;
using System.Collections.Generic;
using System.Linq;
using System.Text;
```

146

```csharp
using System.Threading.Tasks;
using System.Data.Odbc;

namespace NETODBC
{
    class NETODBC
    // Use ODBC connector to retrieve data
    {
        static void Main(string[] args)
        {
            OdbcConnection conn = null;
            OdbcCommand cmd = null;
            OdbcDataReader rdr = null;
            Boolean rows = false;
            int cols = 0;

            try
            {
                conn = new OdbcConnection("DSN=DBHR");
                conn.Open();
                Console.WriteLine("Successful connection!");
                cmd = conn.CreateCommand();
                cmd.CommandText
                = "SELECT EMP_LAST_NAME,"
                + "EMP_FIRST_NAME "
                + "FROM EMPLOYEE "
                + "WHERE EMP_ID = 3217";

                rdr = cmd.ExecuteReader();
                Console.WriteLine("\nExecute: " + cmd.CommandText);

                cols = rdr.FieldCount;
                rows = rdr.HasRows;

                while (rdr.Read() == true)
                {
                    Console.WriteLine("Last name is : " + rdr.GetString(0));

                    Console.WriteLine("First name is : " + rdr.GetString(1));

                }
                rdr.Close();
            }
            catch (Exception e)
            {
                Console.WriteLine(e.Message);
            }

            finally
            {
                Console.WriteLine("Returned Rows? " + rows);
```

```
            conn.Close();
        }

    }
}

}
```

Here's the output:

```
Successful connection!

Execute: SELECT EMP_LAST_NAME,EMP_FIRST_NAME FROM EMPLOYEE WHERE EMP_ID = 3217

Last name is : JOHNSON
First name is : EDWARD
Returned Rows? True
```

.NET PostgreSQL INSERT Program

Before we construct our c# INSERT program, let's first delete the records we added using our Java program so that our .NET examples will work correctly when we add these same records.

```
DELETE FROM EMPLOYEE
WHERE EMP_ID IN (1111, 1112);
```

Now let's construct our INSERT program to add these two rows back. You can use the Visual Studio IDE to create your version of the program. Here I'll just supply the code listing. Let's create solution NETEMP1 and class NETEMP1. Remember to change your application type from Console Application to Windows Application, and to add the PostgreSQL reference.

We'll use the NpgsqlConnection object along with a NpgsqlCommand object. That's all we need. Here is my example code:

```
using System;
using System.Collections.Generic;
using System.Linq;
using System.Text;
using System.Threading.Tasks;
using Npgsql;

/* Program to connect to PostgreSQL and insert a row        */
namespace NETEMP1
{
    class NETEMP1
```

148

```csharp
{
    static void Main(string[] args)
    {
        NpgsqlConnection conn = null;
        NpgsqlCommand cmd = null;

        try
        {
            conn = new NpgsqlConnection("Server=127.0.0.1; Port=5432;
                User ID=postgres; password=postgres; Database=DBHR");

            conn.Open();
            Console.WriteLine("Successful connection!");
            cmd = conn.CreateCommand();
            cmd.CommandText

            = "INSERT INTO EMPLOYEE "
            + "(EMP_ID, "
            + "EMP_LAST_NAME, "
            + "EMP_FIRST_NAME, "
            + "EMP_SERVICE_YEARS, "
            + "EMP_PROMOTION_DATE) "
            + "VALUES (1111, "
            + "'VEREEN', "
            + "'CHARLES', "
            + "12, "
            + "'2017-01-01') ";

            int rowsAffected = cmd.ExecuteNonQuery();
            Console.WriteLine("\n Inserted Rows: " + rowsAffected + " \n");

            /* Now add a second record */
            cmd.CommandText = "INSERT INTO EMPLOYEE "
            + "(EMP_ID, "
            + "EMP_LAST_NAME, "
            + "EMP_FIRST_NAME, "
            + "EMP_SERVICE_YEARS, "
            + "EMP_PROMOTION_DATE) "
            + "VALUES (1112, "
            + "'YATES', "
            + "'JANENE', "
            + "7, "
            + "'2015-01-01') ";

            rowsAffected = cmd.ExecuteNonQuery();
            Console.WriteLine("\n Inserted Rows: " + rowsAffected + " \n");

        }

        catch (Exception e)
        {
            Console.WriteLine(e.Message);
```

```
        }
        finally
        {
            conn.Close();
        }

    }
  }
}
```

Now let's run it, and here is the result:

```
Successful connection!
Inserted Rows: 1
Inserted Rows: 1
```

And we can verify the result by querying the table.

```
SELECT * FROM EMPLOYEE
WHERE EMP_ID IN(1111,1112);
```

EMP_ID	EMP_LAST_NAME	EMP_FIRST_NAME	EMP_SERVICE_YEARS	EMP_PROMOTION_DATE
1111	VEREEN	CHARLES	12	2017-01-01
1112	YATES	JANENE	7	2015-01-01

This is what we expect, so let's move on to the parameter based insert.

.NET PostgreSQL INSERT Program with Parameters

Creating parameters for SQL statements in .NET is somewhat different than in Java but the principle is roughly the same. You can use question marks for the parameter markers or you could use variable names preceded by the @ symbol. We'll use question marks. Then .NET requires you to add parameters by name to the Command object's Parameter collection. First let's change our query to use the ? character as parameter markers.

```
cmd.CommandText = "INSERT INTO EMPLOYEE "
+ "(EMP_ID, "
+ "EMP_LAST_NAME, "
+ "EMP_FIRST_NAME, "
+ "EMP_SERVICE_YEARS, "
+ "EMP_PROMOTION_DATE) "
+ "VALUES (?, "
+ "?, "
+ "?, "
+ "?, "
+ "?);" ;
```

150

Next we use the Add method of the Parameters collection of the Command object to specify parameters and values. In this case we are adding employee 1113 whose name is Rita Duggan with 5 years of service and a promotion date of 1/1/2016.

```
cmd.Parameters.Add(new PostgreSQLParameter("@empid", 1113));
cmd.Parameters.Add(new PostgreSQLParameter("@lname", "DUGGAN"));
cmd.Parameters.Add(new PostgreSQLParameter("@fname", "RITA"));
cmd.Parameters.Add(new PostgreSQLParameter("@yrsofservice", 5));
cmd.Parameters.Add(new PostgreSQLParameter("@promdate",
DateTime.Parse("01/01/2016")));
```

And now we could then execute the query as before.

```
int rowsAffected = cmd.ExecuteNonQuery();
Console.WriteLine("\n Inserted Rows: " + rowsAffected + " \n");
```

But before we run the program, let's add some additional code to change the parameter values and then run the same query again. This is where the value of using parameters comes in. We only need to modify the Value setting of each of our parameters and then perform the command again – no other modification is required. In this case we are adding employee 1114 who is Phyllis Miller with 11 years of service and promotion date 1/1/2017.

```
cmd.Parameters["@empid"].Value = 1114;
cmd.Parameters["@lname"].Value = "MILLER";
cmd.Parameters["@fname"].Value = "PHYLLIS";
cmd.Parameters["@yrsofservice"].Value = 11;
cmd.Parameters["@promdate"].Value = DateTime.Parse("01/01/2017");

rowsAffected = cmd.ExecuteNonQuery();
Console.WriteLine("\n Inserted Rows: " + rowsAffected + " \n");
```

Now we are ready to build the entire modified program and run it to add the two new records. Here's the program listing.

```
using System;
using System.Collections.Generic;
using System.Linq;
using System.Text;
using System.Threading.Tasks;
using Npgsql;

/* Program to connect to PostgreSQL and insert a row      */
```

```csharp
namespace NETEMP1A
{
    class NETEMP1A
    {
        static void Main(string[] args)
        {
            NpgsqlConnection conn = null;
            NpgsqlCommand cmd = null;

            try
            {
                conn = new NpgsqlConnection("Server=127.0.0.1; Port=5432;
                    User ID=postgres; password=postgres; Database=DBHR");
                conn.Open();
                Console.WriteLine("Successful connection!");
                cmd = conn.CreateCommand();

                cmd.CommandText = "INSERT INTO EMPLOYEE "
                + "(EMP_ID, "
                + "EMP_LAST_NAME, "
                + "EMP_FIRST_NAME, "
                + "EMP_SERVICE_YEARS, "
                + "EMP_PROMOTION_DATE) "
                + "VALUES (@empid, "
                + "@lname, "
                + "@fname, "
                + "@yrsofservice, "
                + "@promdate);";

                /*    Now we add parameters to the Command object */

                cmd.Parameters.Add(new NpgsqlParameter("@empid", 1113));
                cmd.Parameters.Add(new NpgsqlParameter("@lname", "DUGGAN"));
                cmd.Parameters.Add(new NpgsqlParameter("@fname", "RITA"));
                cmd.Parameters.Add(new NpgsqlParameter("@yrsofservice", 5));
                cmd.Parameters.Add(new NpgsqlParameter("@promdate",
                DateTime.Parse("2016-01-01")));

                /* Execute the query */

                int rowsAffected = cmd.ExecuteNonQuery();
                Console.WriteLine("\n Inserted Rows: " + rowsAffected
                + " \n");

                /* Update the parameter values and do another insert */

                cmd.Parameters["@empid"].Value = 1114;
                cmd.Parameters["@lname"].Value = "MILLER";
                cmd.Parameters["@fname"].Value = "PHYLLIS";
                cmd.Parameters["@yrsofservice"].Value = 11;
                cmd.Parameters["@promdate"].Value = DateTime.Parse("01/01/2017");
```

```
            rowsAffected = cmd.ExecuteNonQuery();
            Console.WriteLine("\n Inserted Rows: " + rowsAffected
            + "\n");
        }

        catch (Exception e)
        {
            Console.WriteLine(e.Message);
        }

        finally
        {
            conn.Close();
        }

    }
}

}
```

And here is the result:

```
Successful connection!
Inserted Rows: 1
Inserted Rows: 1
```

And we can verify that the records were added by querying the EMPLOYEE table.

```
SELECT * FROM EMPLOYEE
WHERE EMP_ID IN(1113,1114);
```

EMP_ID	EMP_LAST_NAME	EMP_FIRST_NAME	EMP_SERVICE_YEARS	EMP_PROMOTION_DATE
1113	DUGGAN	RITA	5	2016-01-01
1114	MILLER	PHYLLIS	11	2017-01-01

The value of using parameters is that you do not need to rebuild the INSERT statement each time you run the query. You need only change the value of the parameters and then execute the command again. Obviously this model has utility when you are looping through a file of input records, or possibly processing data from another PostgreSQL table or other data source.

OK, now let's move on to an update program.

153

.NET PostgreSQL UPDATE Program

This program will also correct the case on EMP_LAST_NAME as we did with Java, but this is a bit different in .NET. First, let's change all the EMP_LAST_NAME values to lower case.

```
UPDATE EMPLOYEE
SET EMP_LAST_NAME = LOWER(EMP_LAST_NAME);
```

And we can demonstrate that our data is in fact in lower case:

```
SELECT EMP_LAST_NAME FROM EMPLOYEE;

EMP_LAST_NAME
franklin
vereen
jenson
jenkins
duggan
stewart
schultz
yates
johnson
ford
miller
harris
willard
```

In .NET there are several ways to perform PostgreSQL updates such as using an update query with the Command object. Since we want to capture our changes and report them in the console, we're going to use two other objects, which are a NpgsqlDataAdapter and an NpgsqlDataSet.

The DataAdaptor object is used to retrieve data from the EMPLOYEE table and load it to a DataSet. The DataSet is a disconnected copy of the records – we could think of it as a result set. We make changes to the records in the DataSet and then we use the update() method of the DataAdaptor to apply the changes in the Dataset to the table.

Here is our code:

```
using System;
using System.Collections.Generic;
using System.Linq;
using System.Text;
using System.Threading.Tasks;
using System.Data;
using Npgsql;
```

```csharp
namespace NETEMP2
{
    class NETEMP2
    {
        static void Main(string[] args)
        {

            Console.WriteLine("Program NETEMP2 begins successfully");
            NpgsqlConnection conn = new NpgsqlConnection("Server=127.0.0.1;
               Port=5432; User ID=postgres; password=postgres; Database=DBHR");

            DataSet EmployeesDataSet = new DataSet();
            NpgsqlDataAdapter da;
            NpgsqlCommandBuilder cmdBuilder = null;
            try
            {
                conn.Open();
                Console.WriteLine("Successful connection!");

                da = new NpgsqlDataAdapter("SELECT EMP_ID, EMP_LAST_NAME "
                + "FROM EMPLOYEE "
                + "WHERE EMP_LAST_NAME <> UPPER(EMP_LAST_NAME)", conn);

                cmdBuilder = new NpgsqlCommandBuilder(da);
                da.Fill(EmployeesDataSet, "Employees");

                foreach (DataTable DT in EmployeesDataSet.Tables)
                {
                    foreach (DataRow DR in DT.Rows)
                    {
                        string lName = DR[1].ToString();
                        Console.WriteLine("BEFORE surname is " + lName);

                        lName = lName.ToUpper();
                        DR[1] = lName;

                        Console.WriteLine("AFTER surname is " + lName);

                    }

                    // Update the table using values in the dataset

                    da.UpdateCommand = cmdBuilder.GetUpdateCommand();
                    da.Update(EmployeesDataSet, "Employees");
                }

            }

            catch (Exception e)
            {
                Console.WriteLine(e.Message);
```
155

```
        }

    finally
    {
        conn.Close();

        Console.WriteLine("Program NETEMP2 concluded successfully");

    }


        }
    }

}
```

And here is the result:

```
Program NETEMP2 begins successfully
Successful connection!
BEFORE surname is schultz
AFTER surname is SCHULTZ
BEFORE surname is willard
AFTER surname is WILLARD
BEFORE surname is jenkins
AFTER surname is JENKINS
BEFORE surname is ford
AFTER surname is FORD
BEFORE surname is harris
AFTER surname is HARRIS
BEFORE surname is johnson
AFTER surname is JOHNSON
BEFORE surname is stewart
AFTER surname is STEWART
BEFORE surname is franklin
AFTER surname is FRANKLIN
BEFORE surname is vereen
AFTER surname is VEREEN
BEFORE surname is yates
AFTER surname is YATES
BEFORE surname is duggan
AFTER surname is DUGGAN
BEFORE surname is miller
AFTER surname is MILLER
```

The merge and delete functions are given as exercises at the end of the chapter.

COMMIT and ROLLBACK

Central to understanding transaction management is the concept of a unit of work. A unit of work begins when a program is initiated. Multiple adds, changes and deletes may then take place during the same unit of work. The changes are not made permanent until a commit point is reached. A unit of work ends in one of three ways:

1. When a commit is issued.

2. When a rollback is issued.

3. When the program ends. Let's look at each of these.

COMMIT

The COMMIT statement ends a transaction and makes the changes permanent and visible to other processes. Also, when a program ends, there is an implicit COMMIT. This is important to know; however a recommended best practice is to do an explicit COMMIT at the end of the program.

ROLLBACK

A ROLLBACK statement ends a transaction without making changes permanent – the changes are simply discarded. This is done either intentionally by the application when it determines there is a reason to ROLLBACK the changes and it issues a

ROLLBACK is requested explicitly, or it occurs because the system traps an error that requires it to do a ROLLBACK of changes. In both cases, the rolled back changes are those that have been made since the last COMMIT point. If no COMMITs have been issued, then all changes made in the session are rolled back.

Commit Processing

This section concerns the commit, rollback and recovery of an application or application program. Here we'll apply the COMMIT in a PostgreSQL program.

Java Program with Commit

For the PostgreSQL program, we should use the COMMIT statement at appropriate intervals. Let's use our update Java program. Let's set all of our employee records such that the EMP_LAST_NAME is in lower case.

```
UPDATE EMPLOYEE
SET EMP_LAST_NAME = LOWER(EMP_LAST_NAME);
```

```
SELECT EMP_LAST_NAME FROM EMPLOYEE;

EMP_LAST_NAME
franklin
vereen
jenson
jenkins
duggan
stewart
schultz
yates
johnson
ford
miller
harris
willard
```

Ordinarily we'd commit at intervals of hundreds or thousands of records. Since we only have 13 records, let's commit every 5 records. We will set up a commit counter called commitCount and we'll increment it each time we update a record. Once the counter reaches 5 updates, we'll execute the commit method of the connection object. Here is our code:

```
package employee;
import java.sql.*;

public class JAVEMP3 {

        public static void main(String[] args) throws ClassNotFoundException {

                Class.forName("org.postgresql.Driver");
                System.out.println("**** Loaded the JDBC driver");
                String url = "jdbc:postgresql:DBHR?user=postgres&password=postgres";

                Connection con = null;

                try {
                        con = DriverManager.getConnection(url);

                        System.out.println("**** Created the connection");

                        String query = "SELECT EMP_ID, EMP_LAST_NAME " + "FROM EMPLOYEE "
                                        + "WHERE EMP_LAST_NAME <> UPPER(EMP_LAST_NAME)";

                        con.setAutoCommit(false);
```

```java
        Integer recordCount = 0;
        Integer commitCount = 0;

        Integer intEmpNo;
        String strLastName;
        Statement stmt;
        stmt = con.createStatement(ResultSet.TYPE_SCROLL_SENSITIVE,
         ResultSet.CONCUR_UPDATABLE);

        ResultSet rs = stmt.executeQuery(query);

        while (rs.next()) {

            intEmpNo = rs.getInt(1);
            strLastName = rs.getString(2);
            System.out.println("Employee " + intEmpNo
            + " BEFORE Last name is: " + strLastName);
            strLastName = strLastName.toUpperCase();
            rs.updateString(2, strLastName);
            rs.updateRow();
            System.out.println("Employee " + intEmpNo
            + " AFTER      Last name is: " + strLastName);

            recordCount++;
            commitCount++;

            if (commitCount >= 5) {

                con.commit();
                commitCount = 0;
                System.out.println("*** Commit taken at record "
                + recordCount);

            }
        }

        // Do final commit

        con.commit();
        System.out.println("*** Final Commit taken at record "
           + recordCount);

    } catch (SQLException e) {

        System.out.println(e.getMessage());
        System.out.println(e.getErrorCode());
        e.printStackTrace();

    }

}
```

```
}
```

And this is our output:

```
**** Loaded the JDBC driver
**** Created the connection
Employee 3217 BEFORE Last name is: johnson
Employee 3217 AFTER   Last name is: JOHNSON
Employee 7459 BEFORE Last name is: stewart
Employee 7459 AFTER   Last name is: STEWART
Employee 9134 BEFORE Last name is: franklin
Employee 9134 AFTER   Last name is: FRANKLIN
Employee 1111 BEFORE Last name is: vereen
Employee 1111 AFTER   Last name is: VEREEN
Employee 1112 BEFORE Last name is: yates
Employee 1112 AFTER   Last name is: YATES
*** Commit taken at record 5
Employee 1113 BEFORE Last name is: duggan
Employee 1113 AFTER   Last name is: DUGGAN
Employee 1114 BEFORE Last name is: miller
Employee 1114 AFTER   Last name is: MILLER
Employee 4720 BEFORE Last name is: schultz
Employee 4720 AFTER   Last name is: SCHULTZ
Employee 6288 BEFORE Last name is: willard
Employee 6288 AFTER   Last name is: WILLARD
Employee 1122 BEFORE Last name is: jenkins
Employee 1122 AFTER   Last name is: JENKINS
*** Commit taken at record 10
Employee 3333 BEFORE Last name is: ford
Employee 3333 AFTER   Last name is: FORD
Employee 7777 BEFORE Last name is: harris
Employee 7777 AFTER   Last name is: HARRIS
*** Final Commit taken at record 12
```

Sometimes you'll need to adjust the commit counter if it turns out you are not taking commits often enough (which can cause record locking for extended periods of time and potential for deadlock with other programs). Or you might even need to use another measure such as elapsed time instead of record count.

.NET Program with Commit
First let's reset the data to lower case:

```
UPDATE EMPLOYEE
SET EMP_LAST_NAME = LOWER(EMP_LAST_NAME);
```

160

Now, let's fix the data making sure to use commit along the way. A .NET program can commit but it requires using transaction functions associated with the connection object. You can do this using a dataset where you update all the values, and then you do a single commit. Here is an example of how to do this:

```
using System;
using System.Collections.Generic;
using System.Linq;
using System.Text;
using System.Threading.Tasks;
using System.Data;
using Npgsql;

namespace NETEMP3A
{
    class NETEMP3A
    {
        static void Main(string[] args)
        {
            Console.WriteLine("Program NETEMP3A begins successfully");
            NpgsqlConnection conn = new NpgsqlConnection("Server=127.0.0.1;
                Port=5432; User ID=postgres; password=postgres; Database=DBHR");

            DataSet EmployeesDataSet = new DataSet();
            NpgsqlDataAdapter da;
            da = new NpgsqlDataAdapter("SELECT EMP_ID, EMP_LAST_NAME "
            + "FROM EMPLOYEE "
            + "WHERE EMP_LAST_NAME <> UPPER(EMP_LAST_NAME)", conn);

            NpgsqlCommandBuilder cmdBuilder = null;

            try
            {
                conn.Open();
                Console.WriteLine("Successful connection!");

                cmdBuilder = new NpgsqlCommandBuilder(da);

                da.Fill(EmployeesDataSet, "Employees");
                da.SelectCommand.Transaction = conn.BeginTransaction();

                foreach (DataTable DT in EmployeesDataSet.Tables)
                {
                    foreach (DataRow DR in DT.Rows)
                    {
                        string lName = DR[1].ToString();
                        Console.WriteLine("BEFORE surname is " + lName);

                        lName = lName.ToUpper();
                        DR[1] = lName;
```

161

```
                Console.WriteLine("AFTER surname is " + lName);
            }

            // Update the table using values in the dataset

            da.UpdateCommand = cmdBuilder.GetUpdateCommand();
            da.Update(EmployeesDataSet, "Employees");
            da.SelectCommand.Transaction.Commit();
            Console.WriteLine("Transaction Committed");

        }

    }

    catch (Exception e)
    {
        Console.WriteLine(e.Message);
        da.SelectCommand.Transaction.Rollback();
    }

    finally
    {
        conn.Close();
        Console.WriteLine("Program NETEMP3A concluded successfully");

    }

    }
}

}
```

Here's the output:

```
Program NETEMP3A begins successfully
Successful connection!
BEFORE surname is johnson
AFTER surname is JOHNSON
BEFORE surname is stewart
AFTER surname is STEWART
BEFORE surname is franklin
AFTER surname is FRANKLIN
BEFORE surname is vereen
AFTER surname is VEREEN
BEFORE surname is yates
AFTER surname is YATES
BEFORE surname is duggan
AFTER surname is DUGGAN
BEFORE surname is miller
AFTER surname is MILLER
```

```
BEFORE surname is schultz
AFTER surname is SCHULTZ
BEFORE surname is willard
AFTER surname is WILLARD
BEFORE surname is jenkins
AFTER surname is JENKINS
BEFORE surname is ford
AFTER surname is FORD
BEFORE surname is harris
AFTER surname is HARRIS
Transaction Committed
Program NETEMP3A concluded successfully
```

Rollback Processing

ROLLBACK processing simply backs out and discards any pending (uncommitted) changes. You would use it in a program if you encountered an error that required that the program not apply the changes. For example, we included a rollback with our NETEMP3A program in the Catch clause:

```
da.SelectCommand.Transaction.Rollback();
```

Obviously, once you issue a rollback, you can no longer issue a commit on the transaction.

Chapter Four Exercises

For each of the following exercises, you can use either Java or .NET. Or you can do both.

1. Write a Java or .NET program that creates a result set of all employees who have 5 years or more of service from the EMPLOYEE table. Include logic to display any rows that are returned. Display the employee number, last name and first name of these employees.

2. Write a Java or .NET program that tries to insert a record that already exists into the EMPLOYEE table. Your program should capture the error, and your error routine should detail the cause of the error.

3. Write a Java or .NET program to delete employee number 1114.

4. Write a Java or .NET program to merge the following employee information into the EMPLOYEE table.

      Employee Number: 1114
      Employee Last Name :   MILLER
      Employee First Name: PHILLIS
      Employee Years of Service: 11
      Employee Promotion Date: 01/01/2017

      Employee Number: 1115
      Employee Last Name: JENSON
      Employee First Name: PAUL
      Employee Years of Service: 8
      Employee Promotion Date: 01/01/2016

5. Write the Java or .NET code to end a unit of work and make the changes visible to other processes.

6. Write the Java or .NET code to end a unit of work and discard any updates that have been made since the last commit point.

Chapter Five: Testing and Validating Results

You obviously need to test and validate results for new and modified applications. This section is both a reminder to perform structured testing and some hints for how to go about it. If you have been an application developer for very long, most or all of this will not be new to you.

Test Structures

You normally have a test environment which is typically a separate instance of PostgreSQL and is used primarily or exclusively for testing. You or your DBA will create test objects (tables, indexes, views) in the test environment. The DDL is usually saved and then modified as necessary to recreate the same object in another PostgreSQL instance, or to drop and create a new version in the same instance.

If you do both production support and new development activities in the same test environment (not recommended but it's the case in many shops), it is important to have a strategy for dealing with these work flows so they don't impact each other.

For example if you add a column to a table in your test system, that may be fine for the development work. But if someone else is changing the production version of a program (that happens to use the table) to resolve a production problem, it may not work in the test environment because of the new column. Or if it does work in test, when you migrate the fix to production it might not work there. Ideally, use separate test environments for new development and production support.

Test Data

It is vital to know the business rules of the application so that you select a robust set of test data for your application. To test successfully, all branches of your program or package must be tested, and then all components must be tested together (integration testing). It is especially important that in addition to testing new code and SQL, you also perform regression testing on existing code. Take the time to develop a good structured, comprehensive test plan that can be reused many times.

You can create brand new test data, or you can extract data from production and load it to test, or you can do both. Here are a few basic methods for loading test data.

1. Create the data in a flat file and write an application program to load it using INSERT statements.

2. Use the pgAdmin IMPORT and EXPORT utilities to extract data from production and load to test. We'll go over details for this later in this section.

Testing SQL Statements

Before coding SQL statements in an application program, you should test them using pgAdmin. I know this sounds obvious but you can more easily isolate SQL errors in a tool such as pgAdmin than trying to debug embedded code where you don't know whether the problem is the SQL syntax or the program code.

Debugging Programs

When you are getting unexpected results from your program, make sure to review output from the language compiler or interpreter. If you receive any Java or .NET warnings or errors, make sure to resolve them. Often something that appears unimportant may be causing a run time error.

PostgreSQL Export and Import Data Utilities

EXPORT Utility

Use the EXPORT utility to copy the contents of a table into a flat file. To do this, you select the table in the object tree, right click and select the Import/Export option.

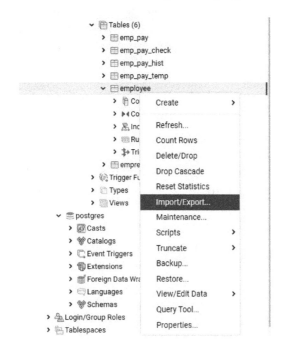

You'll see this screen.

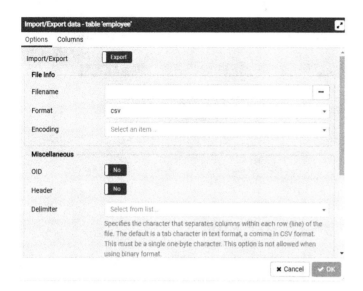

Accept the Export default (this is a switch button that toggles between export and import). Enter a file name for the export, select a format and encoding, and whether you want headers. Also you can select a delimiter character if the default (comma) doesn't work for you. Here are my entries. Now click on the **Columns** tab.

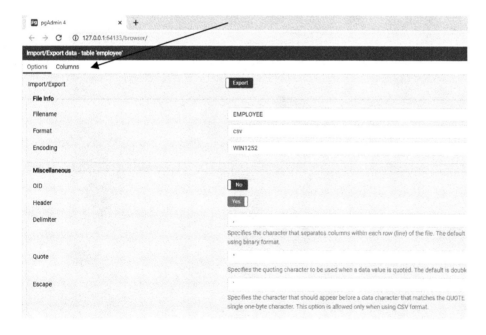

Here you can select any columns that you do not want. In our case, we will keep them all. Click on the **Options** tab.

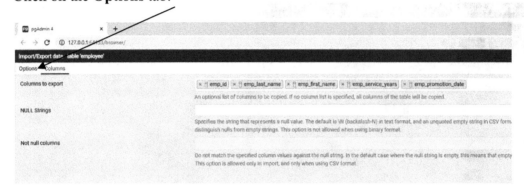

Now validate your file name and other entries and click **Ok**.

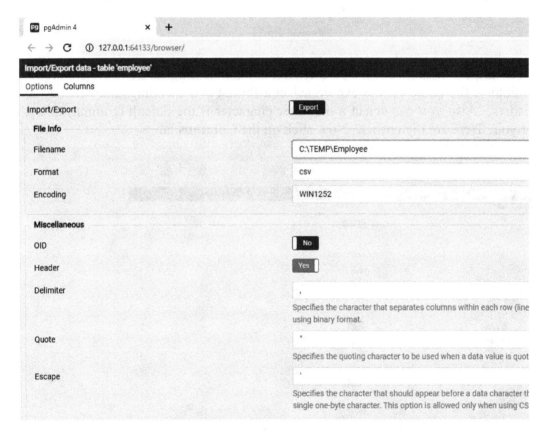

Navigate to your selected folder and open the EMPLOYEE file. Here is mine:

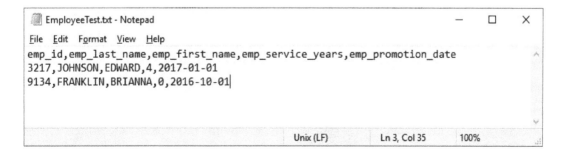

The Export feature is also used to extract data from one system (such as a production system) and load it to another (such as a test system). I recommend that you use it for selecting test data.

IMPORT Data Utility
Use the IMPORT utility when you want to load a PostgreSQL table from an input file. This is useful when you are working in a test system and need to restore a baseline set of data to run through a set of test cases.

To illustrate, let's copy our exported file and edit it down to only two records. Then we can save it as EMPLOYEETEST.

Now let's create a table named EMPLOYEE_TEST. And we'll load the test file to the new table. Here's the DDL for the EMPLOYEE_TEST table:

```
CREATE TABLE EMPLOYEE_TEST
(EMP_ID INT PRIMARY KEY,
EMP_LAST_NAME VARCHAR(30) NOT NULL,
EMP_FIRST_NAME VARCHAR(20) NOT NULL,
EMP_SERVICE_YEARS INT NOT NULL DEFAULT 0,
EMP_PROMOTION_DATE DATE);
```

Now refresh the tables list, right click on EMPLOYEE_TEST and select the Import/Export option. On this screen click on the Export button to toggle it to Import. Enter the file name, encoding, whether or not there are column headers in the file, and the field delimiter character. Then click **Ok.**

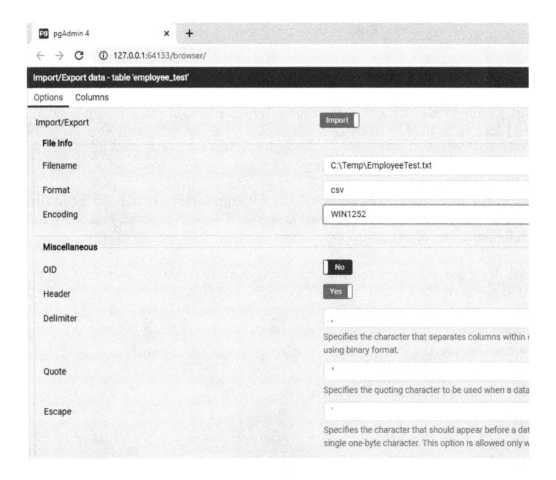

Then you can run a query to see the data in the EMPLOYEE_TEST table. As you can see, it matches the records that we used for the import file.

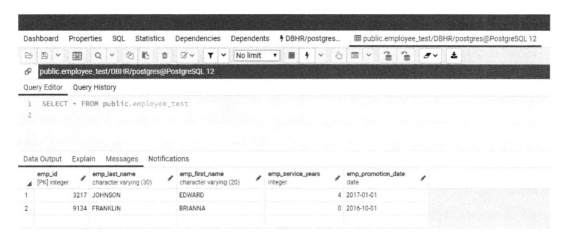

Again the Import utility is most useful for running testing where you need to reload the same data. I recommend you use it often in both development and maintenance environments.

APPENDICES

Appendix One: Answers for Chapter Exercises

Chapter Two Exercises

1. Write a DDL statement to create a base table named EMP_DEPENDENT under user DBHR. The columns should be named as follows and have the specified attributes. There is no primary key.

Field Name	Type	Attributes
EMP_ID	INTEGER	NOT NULL, PRIMARY KEY
EMP_DEP_LAST_NAME	VARCHAR(30)	NOT NULL
EMP_DEP_FIRST_NAME	VARCHAR(20)	NOT NULL
EMP_RELATIONSHIP	VARCHAR(15)	NOT NULL

```
CREATE TABLE EMP_DEPENDENT
(EMP_ID INT NOT NULL,
 EMP_DEP_LAST_NAME VARCHAR(30) NOT NULL,
 EMP_DEP_FIRST_NAME VARCHAR(20) NOT NULL,
 EMP_DEP_RELATIONSHIP VARCHAR(15) NOT NULL);
```

You can add data to the table and retrieve it as follows:

```
INSERT INTO EMP_DEPENDENT
VALUES(3217,'JOHNSON','ELENA','WIFE');

SELECT * FROM EMP_DEPENDENT;

EMP_ID   EMP_DEP_LAST_NAME   EMP_DEP_FIRST_NAME   EMP_DEP_RELATIONSHIP
3217     JOHNSON             ELENA                WIFE
```

2. Create a statement to create a referential constraint on table EMP_DEPENDENT such that only employee ids which exist on the EMPLOYEE table can have an entry in EMP_DEPENDENT. If there is an attempt to delete an EMPLOYEE record that has EMP_DEPENDENT records associated with it, then do not allow the delete to take place.

```
ALTER TABLE EMP_DEPENDENT
ADD CONSTRAINT FK_EMP_DEPENDENT
FOREIGN KEY (EMP_ID) REFERENCES EMPLOYEE (EMP_ID);
```

```
DELETE FROM EMPLOYEE WHERE EMP_ID = 3217;
```

ERROR: update or delete on table "employee" violates foreign key constraint "fk_emp_dependent" on table "emp_dependent" DETAIL: Key (emp_id)=(3217) is still referenced from table "emp_dependent".

Chapter Three Exercises

1. Write a query to display the last and first names of all employees in the EMPLOYEE table. Display the names in alphabetic order by EMP_LAST_NAME.

```
SELECT EMP_LAST_NAME, EMP_FIRST_NAME
FROM EMPLOYEE
ORDER BY EMP_LAST_NAME;
```

2. Write a query to change the first name of Edward Johnson (employee 3217) to Eddie.

```
UPDATE EMPLOYEE
SET EMP_FIRST_NAME = 'EDDIE'
WHERE EMP_ID = 3217;
```

3. Write a query to produce the number of employees in the EMPLOYEE table.

```
SELECT COUNT(*)
FROM EMPLOYEE;
```

Chapter Four Exercises

1. Write a Java or .NET program that creates a result set of all employees who have 5 years or more of service from the EMPLOYEE table. Include logic to display any rows that are returned. Display the employee number, last name and first name of these employees.

Java Solution:

```
package employee;
import java.sql.*;

public class JAVEMP4 {

        public static void main(String[] args) throws ClassNotFoundException {

                Class.forName("org.postgresql.Driver");
                System.out.println("**** Loaded the JDBC driver");
                String url
                  = "jdbc:postgresql:DBHR?user=postgres&password=postgres";
                Connection con = null;

                try {
                        con = DriverManager.getConnection(url, user, password);
                        System.out.println("**** Created the connection");

                        String query = "SELECT EMP_ID, " + "EMP_LAST_NAME,"
                            + "EMP_FIRST_NAME " + "FROM EMPLOYEE "
                            + "WHERE EMP_SERVICE_YEARS >= 5";

                        Statement stmt;
                        stmt = con.createStatement();
                        ResultSet rs = stmt.executeQuery(query);
                        while (rs.next()) {
                                int intEmpId = rs.getInt(1);
                                String strLastName = rs.getString(2);
                                String strFirstName = rs.getString(3);
                                System.out.println("EMP_ID is "
                                    + intEmpId
                                    + " Last name is "
                                    + strLastName
                                    + " First name is "
                                    + strFirstName);
                        }

                } catch (SQLException e) {
                        System.out.println(e.getMessage());
```

```
                              System.out.println(e.getErrorCode());
                              e.printStackTrace();

                    }

              }

       }
```

Output is:

```
**** Loaded the JDBC driver
**** Created the connection
EMP_ID is 4720 Last name is SCHULTZ First name is TIM
EMP_ID is 6288 Last name is WILLARD First name is JOE
EMP_ID is 1122 Last name is JENKINS First name is DEBORAH
EMP_ID is 3333 Last name is FORD First name is JAMES
EMP_ID is 1111 Last name is VEREEN First name is CHARLES
EMP_ID is 1112 Last name is YATES First name is JANENE
EMP_ID is 7459 Last name is STEWART First name is BETTY
```

.NET Solution:

```csharp
using System;
using System.Collections.Generic;
using System.Linq;
using System.Text;
using System.Threading.Tasks;
using Npgsql;

namespace EMPLOYEE
{
    class NETEMP4
    {
        static void Main(string[] args)
        {
            NpgsqlConnection conn = null;
            NpgsqlCommand cmd = null;
            NpgsqlDataReader rdr = null;
            Boolean rows = false;
            int cols = 0;

            try
            {
                conn = new NpgsqlConnection("Server=127.0.0.1; Port=5432;
                    User ID=postgres; password=postgres; Database=DBHR");
                conn.Open();
                Console.WriteLine("Successful connection!");
```

177

```
        cmd = conn.CreateCommand();
        cmd.CommandText
        = "SELECT EMP_ID,"
        + "EMP_LAST_NAME, "
        + "EMP_FIRST_NAME "
        + "FROM EMPLOYEE "
        + "WHERE EMP_SERVICE_YEARS >=5 ";

        rdr = cmd.ExecuteReader();
        Console.WriteLine("\nExecute: " + cmd.CommandText);

        cols = rdr.FieldCount;
        rows = rdr.HasRows;

        while (rdr.Read() == true)
        {
            Console.WriteLine("EMP_ID is : " + rdr.GetInt32(0)
            + " Last name is : " + rdr.GetString(1)
            + "  First name is : " + rdr.GetString(2));
        }

    }

    catch (Exception e)
    {
        Console.WriteLine(e.Message);
    }

    finally
    {
        Console.WriteLine("Returned Rows? " + rows);
        conn.Close();
    }

    }
}

}
```

The output is:

```
Successful connection!

Execute:  SELECT   EMP_ID,EMP_LAST_NAME,  EMP_FIRST_NAME   FROM   EMPLOYEE   WHERE
EMP_SERVICE_YEARS >=5
EMP_ID is : 7459 Last name is : STEWART  First name is : BETTY
EMP_ID is : 1111 Last name is : VEREEN  First name is : CHARLES
EMP_ID is : 1112 Last name is : YATES   First name is : JANENE
EMP_ID is : 1113 Last name is : DUGGAN  First name is : RITA
EMP_ID is : 1114 Last name is : MILLER  First name is : PHYLLIS
EMP_ID is : 4720 Last name is : SCHULTZ  First name is : TIM
```

```
EMP_ID is : 6288 Last name is : WILLARD  First name is : JOE
EMP_ID is : 1122 Last name is : JENKINS  First name is : DEBORAH
EMP_ID is : 3333 Last name is : FORD  First name is : JAMES
Returned Rows? True
```

2. Write a Java or .NET program that tries to insert a record that already exists into the
    EMPLOYEE table. Your program should capture the error, and your error routine should
    detail the cause of the error.

Java Solution:

```java
package employee;

import java.sql.*;

public class JAVEMP1 {

        public static void main(String[] args) throws ClassNotFoundException {

                Class.forName("org.postgresql.Driver");
                System.out.println("**** Loaded the JDBC driver");
                String url = "jdbc:postgresql:DBHR?user=postgres&password=postgres";

                Connection con = null;

                try {
                        con = DriverManager.getConnection(url, user, password);
                        System.out.println("**** Created the connection");

                        String query = "INSERT INTO EMPLOYEE " + "(EMP_ID, "
                            + "EMP_LAST_NAME, "
                            + "EMP_FIRST_NAME, "
                            + "EMP_SERVICE_YEARS, "
                            + "EMP_PROMOTION_DATE) "
                            + "VALUES (1111, "
                            + "'VEREEN', "
                            + "'CHARLES', "
                            + "12, "
                            + "'2017-01-01') ";

                        Statement stmt;
                        stmt = con.createStatement();
                        stmt.executeUpdate(query);
                        System.out.println("Successful INSERT of employee " + 1111);

                } catch (SQLException e) {
                        System.out.println(e.getMessage());
                        System.out.println(e.getErrorCode());
                        e.printStackTrace();
```

179

```
                }

          }

}
```

The output is:

```
**** Loaded the JDBC driver
**** Created the connection
ERROR: duplicate key value violates unique constraint "employee_pkey"
  Detail: Key (emp_id)=(1111) already exists.
```

.NET Solution:

```csharp
using System;
using System.Collections.Generic;
using System.Linq;
using System.Text;
using System.Threading.Tasks;
using Npgsql;

/* Program to connect to PostgreSQL and insert a row        */
namespace NETEMP1
{
    class NETEMP1
    {
        static void Main(string[] args)
        {
            NpgsqlConnection conn = null;
            NpgsqlCommand cmd = null;

            try
            {
                conn = new NpgsqlConnection("Server=127.0.0.1; Port=5432;
                        User ID=postgres; password=postgres; Database=DBHR");

                conn.Open();
                Console.WriteLine("Successful connection!");
                cmd = conn.CreateCommand();
                cmd.CommandText

                = "INSERT INTO EMPLOYEE "
                + "(EMP_ID, "
                + "EMP_LAST_NAME, "
                + "EMP_FIRST_NAME, "
                + "EMP_SERVICE_YEARS, "
                + "EMP_PROMOTION_DATE) "
```

```
                + "VALUES (1111, "
                + "'VEREEN', "
                + "'CHARLES', "
                + "12, "
                + "'2017-01-01') ";

                int rowsAffected = cmd.ExecuteNonQuery();
                Console.WriteLine("\n Inserted Rows: " + rowsAffected + " \n");

                /* Now add a second record */
                cmd.CommandText = "INSERT INTO EMPLOYEE "
                + "(EMP_ID, "
                + "EMP_LAST_NAME, "
                + "EMP_FIRST_NAME, "
                + "EMP_SERVICE_YEARS, "
                + "EMP_PROMOTION_DATE) "
                + "VALUES (1112, "
                + "'YATES', "
                + "'JANENE', "
                + "7, "
                + "'2015-01-01') ";

                rowsAffected = cmd.ExecuteNonQuery();
                Console.WriteLine("\n Inserted Rows: " + rowsAffected + " \n");

            }

            catch (Exception e)
            {
                Console.WriteLine(e.Message);
            }

            finally
            {
                conn.Close();
            }

        }
    }
}
```

The output is:

```
Successful connection!

Exception thrown: 'Npgsql.PostgresException' in mscorlib.dll
23505: duplicate key value violates unique constraint "employee_pkey"
```

3. Write a Java or .NET program to delete employee numbers 1113 and 1114.

Java Solution:

Note: These employee ids were added by NETEMP1A. If you did not run that program, you'll need to before this exercise will work. You can also add these employee ids manually if you prefer.

There are a few ways to do this in Java. We could simply create a statement object and run the SQL. In this case, let's create a result set so that we can record the actions and the employee numbers that we are deleting.

```java
package employee;
import java.sql.*;
public class JAVEMP5 {

        public static void main(String[] args) throws ClassNotFoundException {

                Class.forName("org.postgresql.Driver");
                System.out.println("**** Loaded the JDBC driver");
                String url = "jdbc:postgresql:DBHR?user=postgres&password=postgres";

                Connection con = null;

                try {
                        con = DriverManager.getConnection(url, user, password);
                        System.out.println("**** Created the connection");

                        String query = "SELECT EMP_ID, EMP_LAST_NAME "
                           + "FROM EMPLOYEE " + "WHERE EMP_ID IN (1113, 1114)";

                        Integer intEmpNo;
                        String strLastName;
                        Statement stmt;
                        Stmt = con.createStatement(ResultSet.TYPE_SCROLL_SENSITIVE,
                                ResultSet.CONCUR_UPDATABLE);

                        ResultSet rs = stmt.executeQuery(query);
                        while (rs.next()) {
                                intEmpNo = rs.getInt(1);
                                strLastName = rs.getString(2);
                                rs.deleteRow();
                                System.out.println("Employee " + intEmpNo
                                   + " Last name is: "
                                   + strLastName + " has been deleted");
                        }
                        con.commit();

                }
```

182

```
        catch (SQLException e) {
                System.out.println(e.getMessage());
                System.out.println(e.getErrorCode());
                e.printStackTrace();

        }

        finally {

                System.out.println("** JAVEMP2 finished");
        }

    }

}
```

Output is:

```
**** Loaded the JDBC driver
**** Created the connection
Employee 1113 Last name is: DUGGAN has been deleted
Employee 1114 Last name is: MILLER has been deleted
** JAVEMP5 finished
```

.NET Solution:

If you ran the Java version of the program, you'll need to add employees 1113 and 1114 back before we can delete them. You can do this by executing NETEMP1A.

Now let's look at NETEMP5 which will delete these records again.

```
using System;
using System.Collections.Generic;
using System.Linq;
using System.Text;
using System.Threading.Tasks;
using System.Data;
using PostgreSQL.Client.Provider;


namespace NETEMP5
{
    class NETEMP5
    {
        static void Main(string[] args)
```
183

```
{
    Console.WriteLine("Program NETEMP5 begins successfully");
    NpgsqlConnection conn = new NpgsqlConnection("Data Source = 192.168.1.155;
       User ID = 'DBHR'; Password = 'DBHR';");

    DataSet EmployeesDataSet = new DataSet();
    NpgsqlDataAdapter da;
    NpgsqlCommandBuilder cmdBuilder = null;

    try
    {
        conn.Open();
        Console.WriteLine("Successful connection!");

        da = new NpgsqlDataAdapter("SELECT EMP_ID, EMP_LAST_NAME "
        + "FROM EMPLOYEE "
        + "WHERE EMP_ID IN (1113, 1114)", conn);

        cmdBuilder = new NpgsqlCommandBuilder(da);

        da.Fill(EmployeesDataSet, "Employees");

        foreach (DataTable DT in EmployeesDataSet.Tables)
        {
            foreach (DataRow DR in DT.Rows)
            {
                string empId = DR[0].ToString();
                string lName = DR[1].ToString();
                Console.WriteLine("Employee "
                    + empId
                    + " Last Name "
                    + lName + " is being deleted");

                DR.Delete();

            }

            // Update the table using the delete actions in the dataset

            da.UpdateCommand = cmdBuilder.GetUpdateCommand();
            da.Update(EmployeesDataSet, "Employees");
        }

    }

    catch (Exception e)
    {
        Console.WriteLine(e.Message);
    }

    finally
    {
```

184

```
            conn.Close();
            Console.WriteLine("Program NETEMP5 concluded successfully");

        }

    }

}

}
```

The output is:

```
Successful connection!
Employee 1113 Last Name DUGGAN is being deleted
Employee 1114 Last Name MILLER is being deleted
Program NETEMP5 concluded successfully
```

4. Write a Java or .NET program to merge the following employee information into the
    EMPLOYEE table.

```
Employee Number:              1114
Employee Last Name:           MILLER
Employee First Name:          PHILLIS
Employee Years of Service :   11
Employee Promotion Date:      01/01/2017

Employee Number:              1115
Employee Last Name:           JENSON
Employee First Name:          PAUL
Employee Years of Service :   8
Employee Promotion Date:      01/01/2016
```

Java Solution:

Since PostgreSQL has no merge statement, we will use an INSERT with the On Conflict
Do Update feature. We'll execute two SQL statements as follows:

```
INSERT INTO EMPLOYEE AS T
(EMP_ID,
 EMP_LAST_NAME,
 EMP_FIRST_NAME,
 EMP_SERVICE_YEARS,
 EMP_PROMOTION_DATE)
VALUES (1114,
'MILLER',
'PHYLLIS',
11,
'2017-01-01')
```

185

```
ON CONFLICT (EMP_ID) DO UPDATE
SET EMP_LAST_NAME      = EXCLUDED.EMP_LAST_NAME,
    EMP_FIRST_NAME     = EXCLUDED.EMP_FIRST_NAME,
    EMP_SERVICE_YEARS  = EXCLUDED.EMP_SERVICE_YEARS,
    EMP_PROMOTION_DATE = EXCLUDED.EMP_PROMOTION_DATE
    WHERE T.EMP_ID     = EXCLUDED.EMP_ID;

INSERT INTO EMPLOYEE AS T
(EMP_ID,
 EMP_LAST_NAME,
 EMP_FIRST_NAME,
 EMP_SERVICE_YEARS,
 EMP_PROMOTION_DATE)
VALUES (1115,
'JENSON',
'PAUL',
8,
'2016-01-01')

ON CONFLICT (EMP_ID) DO UPDATE
SET EMP_LAST_NAME      = EXCLUDED.EMP_LAST_NAME,
    EMP_FIRST_NAME     = EXCLUDED.EMP_FIRST_NAME,
    EMP_SERVICE_YEARS  = EXCLUDED.EMP_SERVICE_YEARS,
    EMP_PROMOTION_DATE = EXCLUDED.EMP_PROMOTION_DATE
    WHERE T.EMP_ID     = EXCLUDED.EMP_ID;
```

Here is the program code:

```java
package employee;
import java.sql.*;

public class JAVEMP6 {

    public static void main(String[] args) throws ClassNotFoundException {

        Class.forName("org.postgresql.Driver");
        System.out.println("**** Loaded the JDBC driver");
        String url = "jdbc:postgresql:DBHR?user=postgres&password=postgres";
        Connection con = null;

        try {
            con = DriverManager.getConnection(url);
            System.out.println("**** Created the connection");
            String query = "INSERT INTO EMPLOYEE AS T"
            + " (EMP_ID, EMP_LAST_NAME, EMP_FIRST_NAME, "
            + "EMP_SERVICE_YEARS, EMP_PROMOTION_DATE) "
            + " VALUES (1114, 'MILLER', 'PHYLLIS', 11, '2017-01-01') "
            + " ON CONFLICT (EMP_ID) DO UPDATE "
            + "SET EMP_LAST_NAME = EXCLUDED.EMP_LAST_NAME, "
```

```
                   + "EMP_FIRST_NAME = EXCLUDED.EMP_FIRST_NAME, "
                   + "EMP_SERVICE_YEARS = EXCLUDED.EMP_SERVICE_YEARS, "
                   + "EMP_PROMOTION_DATE = EXCLUDED.EMP_PROMOTION_DATE "
                   + " WHERE T.EMP_ID = EXCLUDED.EMP_ID; ";

             Statement stmt;
             stmt = con.createStatement();
             stmt.executeUpdate(query);

             System.out.println("Successful MERGE of employee 1114");

             query = "INSERT INTO EMPLOYEE AS T"
             + " (EMP_ID, EMP_LAST_NAME, EMP_FIRST_NAME, "
             + "EMP_SERVICE_YEARS, EMP_PROMOTION_DATE) "
             + " VALUES (1115, 'JENSON', 'PAUL', 8, '2016-01-01') "
             + " ON CONFLICT (EMP_ID) DO UPDATE "
             + "SET EMP_LAST_NAME = EXCLUDED.EMP_LAST_NAME, "
             + "EMP_FIRST_NAME = EXCLUDED.EMP_FIRST_NAME, "
             + "EMP_SERVICE_YEARS = EXCLUDED.EMP_SERVICE_YEARS, "
             + "EMP_PROMOTION_DATE = EXCLUDED.EMP_PROMOTION_DATE "
             + " WHERE T.EMP_ID = EXCLUDED.EMP_ID; ";

             stmt.executeUpdate(query);
             System.out.println("Successful MERGE of employee 1115");

       } catch (SQLException e) {
             System.out.println(e.getMessage());
             System.out.println(e.getErrorCode());
             e.printStackTrace();

       }

   }

}
```

The output is:

```
**** Loaded the JDBC driver
**** Created the connection
Successful MERGE of employee 1114
Successful MERGE of employee 1115
```

.NET Solution:

If you did the Java example, first delete record 1115 before running the .NET program.

```
DELETE FROM EMPLOYEE
WHERE EMP_ID = 1115;
```

```csharp
using System;
using System.Collections.Generic;
using System.Linq;
using System.Text;
using System.Threading.Tasks;
using Npgsql;

namespace NETEMP6
{
    class NETEMP6
    {
        static void Main(string[] args)
        {
            NpgsqlConnection conn = null;
            NpgsqlCommand cmd = null;

            try
            {
            conn = new NpgsqlConnection("Server=127.0.0.1; Port=5432;
               User ID=postgres; password=postgres; Database=DBHR");
            conn.Open(); Console.WriteLine("Successful connection!");
            cmd = conn.CreateCommand();
            cmd.CommandText = "INSERT INTO EMPLOYEE AS T"
            + " (EMP_ID, EMP_LAST_NAME, EMP_FIRST_NAME, "
            + "EMP_SERVICE_YEARS, EMP_PROMOTION_DATE) "
            + " VALUES (1114, 'MILLER', 'PHYLLIS', 11, '2017-01-01') "
            + " ON CONFLICT (EMP_ID) DO UPDATE "
            + "SET EMP_LAST_NAME = EXCLUDED.EMP_LAST_NAME, "
            + "EMP_FIRST_NAME = EXCLUDED.EMP_FIRST_NAME, "
            + "EMP_SERVICE_YEARS = EXCLUDED.EMP_SERVICE_YEARS, "
            + "EMP_PROMOTION_DATE = EXCLUDED.EMP_PROMOTION_DATE "
            + " WHERE T.EMP_ID = EXCLUDED.EMP_ID; ";

            int rowsAffected = cmd.ExecuteNonQuery();
            Console.WriteLine("\n Merged Rows: " + rowsAffected + " \n");

            cmd.CommandText = "INSERT INTO EMPLOYEE AS T"
            + " (EMP_ID, EMP_LAST_NAME, EMP_FIRST_NAME, "
            + "EMP_SERVICE_YEARS, EMP_PROMOTION_DATE) "
            + " VALUES (1115, 'JENSON', 'PAUL', 8, '2016-01-01') "
            + " ON CONFLICT (EMP_ID) DO UPDATE "
            + "SET EMP_LAST_NAME = EXCLUDED.EMP_LAST_NAME, "
            + "EMP_FIRST_NAME = EXCLUDED.EMP_FIRST_NAME, "
            + "EMP_SERVICE_YEARS = EXCLUDED.EMP_SERVICE_YEARS, "
            + "EMP_PROMOTION_DATE = EXCLUDED.EMP_PROMOTION_DATE "
            + " WHERE T.EMP_ID = EXCLUDED.EMP_ID; ";

            rowsAffected = cmd.ExecuteNonQuery();
```

188

```
                Console.WriteLine("\n Merged Rows: " + rowsAffected + " \n");

            }

            catch (Exception e)
            {
                Console.WriteLine(e.Message);
            }

            finally
            {
                conn.Close();
            }

        }
    }
}
```

The output is:

```
Successful connection!
Merged Rows: 1
Merged Rows: 1
```

5. Write the Java or .NET code to end a unit of work and make the changes visible to other processes.

Assuming a NpgsqlConnection object named "conn":

In Java:

```
con.commit();
```

In .NET:

You have to use the transaction object to issue a commit. Assuming a connection named conn:

```
NpsqlTransaction tran = null;
tran = conn.BeginTransaction();

// DO SOME UPDATES HERE

tran.Commit();
```

6. Write the Java or .NET code to end a unit of work and discard any updates that have been made since the last commit point.

Assuming a NpsqlConnection object named "conn":

In Java:

```
conn.rollback();
```

In .NET:

You have to use the transaction object to issue a rollback.

```
NpgsqlTransaction tran = null;
tran = conn.BeginTransaction();


// DO SOME UPDATES HERE

tran.Rollback();
```

Appendix Two – Install Instructions for Java and .NET IDEs

Eclipse Java Oxygen

Eclipse is a free, open source IDE that you can use to build Java programs. I find it easy to use, and I recommend that you download and install it if you are not already using another Java IDE (such as NetBeans).

In this text book we've shown a basic example of creating a Java program in the Eclipse IDE, but we didn't spend time showing all its features. There is plenty of user reference material on Eclipse elsewhere.

```
http://help.eclipse.org/oxygen/index.jsp
```

To acquire and install Eclipse Java Oxygen, go to this site:

```
https://www.eclipse.org/downloads/download.php?file=/oomph/epp/oxygen/R2/eclipse-inst-win64.exe
```

Select the option for Eclipse Oxygen. Click on the **Download** button. Assuming you chose the download for a 64-bit Windows machine, you'll download this file:

```
eclipse-inst-win64.exe
```

When you open this file you will see the Eclipse installer. Select the Eclipse IDE for Java Developers by clicking on it.

eclipseinstaller by Oomph

type filter text 🔍

Eclipse IDE for Java Developers

The essential tools for any Java developer, including a Java IDE, a Git client, XML Editor, Mylyn, Maven and Gradle integration

Eclipse IDE for Enterprise Java Developers

Tools for Java developers creating Enterprise Java and Web applications, including a Java IDE, tools for Enterprise Java, JPA, JSF, Mylyn, Maven, Git and...

Eclipse IDE for C/C++ Developers

An IDE for C/C++ developers with Mylyn integration.

Eclipse IDE for JavaScript and Web Developers (includes in

The essential tools for any JavaScript developer, including JavaScript, TypeScript, HTML, CSS, XML, Yaml, Markdown... languages support; Kubernetes, Angular...

Eclipse IDE for PHP Developers

The essential tools for any PHP developer, including PHP language support, Git client, Mylyn and editors for JavaScript, HTML, CSS and XML.

When you see the Eclipse Installer window, click on the INSTALL button. Wait a few minutes while the installer runs.

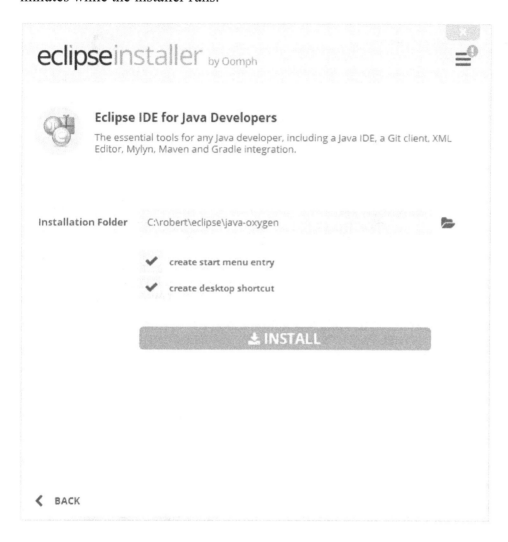

Accept the user agreement.

Eclipse Installer — □ ×

Eclipse Foundation Software User Agreement

Applicable licenses will be discovered and prompted later in the installation process. Avoid such interruptions by accepting the most common license now.

Oomph

Eclipse Foundation Software User Agreement

April 9, 2014

Usage Of Content

THE ECLIPSE FOUNDATION MAKES AVAILABLE SOFTWARE, DOCUMENTATION, INFORMATION AND/OR OTHER MATERIALS FOR OPEN SOURCE PROJECTS (COLLECTIVELY "CONTENT"). USE OF THE CONTENT IS GOVERNED BY THE TERMS AND CONDITIONS OF THIS AGREEMENT AND/OR THE TERMS AND CONDITIONS OF LICENSE AGREEMENTS OR NOTICES INDICATED OR REFERENCED BELOW. BY USING THE CONTENT, YOU AGREE THAT YOUR USE OF THE CONTENT IS GOVERNED BY THIS AGREEMENT AND/OR THE TERMS AND CONDITIONS OF ANY APPLICABLE LICENSE AGREEMENTS OR NOTICES INDICATED OR REFERENCED BELOW. IF YOU DO NOT AGREE TO THE TERMS AND CONDITIONS OF THIS AGREEMENT AND THE TERMS AND CONDITIONS OF ANY APPLICABLE LICENSE AGREEMENTS OR NOTICES INDICATED OR REFERENCED BELOW, THEN YOU MAY NOT USE THE CONTENT.

Applicable Licenses

Unless otherwise indicated, all Content made available by the Eclipse Foundation is provided to you under the terms and conditions of the Eclipse Public License Version 1.0 ("EPL"). A copy of the EPL is provided with this Content and is also available at http://www.eclipse.org/legal/epl-v10.html. For purposes of the EPL, "Program" will mean the Content.

Content includes, but is not limited to, source code, object code, documentation and other files maintained in the Eclipse Foundation source code repository ("Repository") in software modules

Accept Now   Decide Later

Monitor the install.

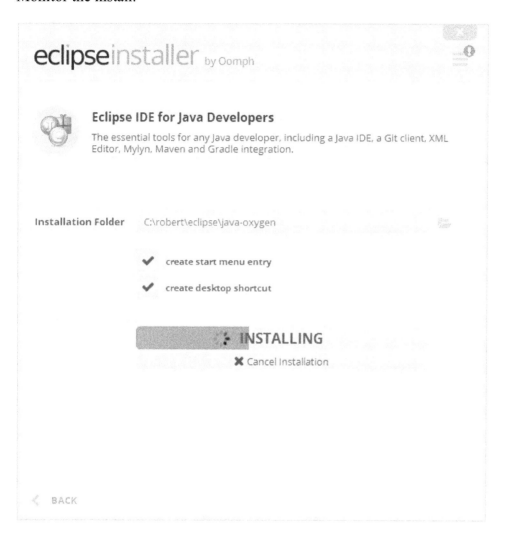

eclipseinstaller by Oomph

Eclipse IDE for Java Developers

The essential tools for any Java developer, including a Java IDE, a Git client, XML Editor, Mylyn, Maven and Gradle integration.

Installation Folder   C:\robert\eclipse\java-oxygen

✔   create start menu entry

✔   create desktop shortcut

⚙ **INSTALLING**

✖ Cancel Installation

‹ BACK

Accept the license confirmation. The install will continue.

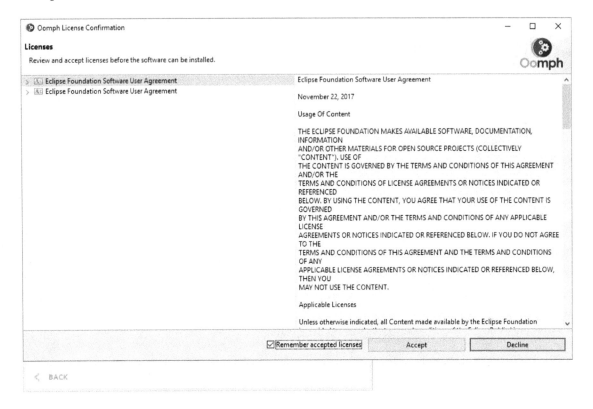

You'll need to specify a work space – I am using a folder named **robert**. Now you can either click on the Launch button, or come back later and use the desktop icon (or the Eclipse entry from your program launcher).

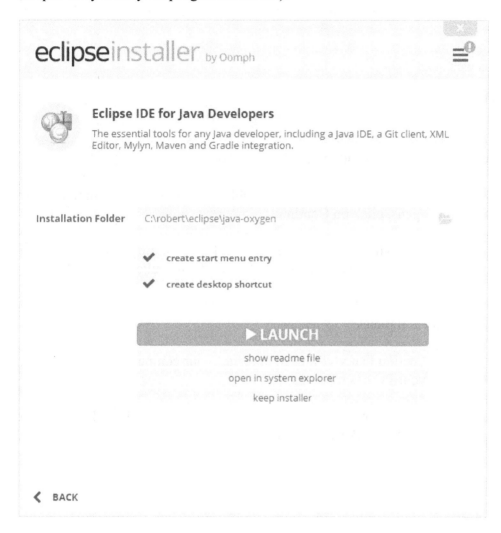

Now you'll see the Eclipse IDE.

Visual Studio Community

Microsoft provides a free "community" version of its Visual Studio IDE for use with .NET. We'll show coding examples using the c# .NET language. If you are following along and doing the examples and want to use .NET, you may want to install this free IDE.

Navigate to this web site:

https://www.visualstudio.com/vs/community/

Click on Download Visual Studio and follow the instructions.

Next, go to the folder you downloaded into, and double click on the VS Community.exe file. In the window that opens, click on Continue.

You'll arrive at this window where you can select a "workload" setting. For our purposes in this text book, we can choose .NET desktop development. Then click on Install.

It will take a while to install the software. You might want to take a break. You'll see this window when the install completes:

You may also see a notification that you'll need to restart your computer. If so, then click on Restart. Return after your PC has rebooted.

Once you've rebooted, you can open Visual Studio from the Programs List. There will be a short delay while first-time housekeeping is done.

Finally you'll see the initial IDE window.

INDEX

Other Titles by Robert Wingate

PostgreSQL Basic Training for Application Developers

ISBN-13: 978-1082748882

This book will help you learn the basic information and skills you need to develop applications with Teradata. The instruction, examples and questions/answers in this book are a fast track to becoming productive as quickly as possible. The content is easy to read and digest, well organized and focused on honing real job skills. Programming examples are coded in both Java and C# .NET. Teradata Basic Training for Application Developers is a key step in the direction of mastering Teradata application development so you'll be ready to join a technical team.

ISBN-13: 978-1793440433

This book will teach you the basic information and skills you need to develop applications with IMS on IBM mainframe computers running z/OS. The instruction, examples and sample programs in this book are a fast track to becoming productive as quickly as possible using IMS with COBOL and PLI. The content is easy to read and digest, well organized and focused on honing real job skills.

ISBN-13: 978-1986039840

This book will teach you the basic information and skills you need to develop applications on IBM mainframes running z/OS. The instruction, examples and sample programs in this book are a fast track to becoming productive as quickly as possible in JCL, MVS Utilities, COBOL, PLI and DB2. The content is easy to read and digest, well organized and focused on honing real job skills. IBM z/OS Quick Start Training for Application Developers is a key step in the direction of mastering IBM application development so you'll be ready to join a technical team.

ISBN-13: 978-1717284594

This book will teach you the basic information and skills you need to develop applications on IBM mainframes running z/OS. The instruction, examples and sample programs in this book are a fast track to becoming productive as quickly as possible in VSAM, IMS and DB2. The content is easy to read and digest, well organized and focused on honing real job skills. IBM z/OS Quick Start Training for Application Developers is a key step in the direction of mastering IBM application development so you'll be ready to join a technical team.

Additional titles are on the following pages.

DB2 Exam C2090-313 Preparation Guide

ISBN 13: 978-1548463052

This book will help you pass IBM Exam C2090-313 and become an IBM Certified Application Developer - DB2 11 for z/OS. The instruction, examples and questions/answers in the book offer you a significant advantage by helping you to gauge your readiness for the exam, to better understand the objectives being tested, and to get a broad exposure to the DB2 11 knowledge you'll be tested on.

DB2 Exam C2090-320 Preparation Guide

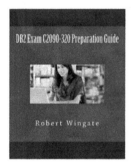

ISBN 13: 978-1544852096

This book will help you pass IBM Exam C2090-320 and become an IBM Certified Database Associate - DB2 11 Fundamentals for z/OS. The instruction, examples and questions/answers in the book offer you a significant advantage by helping you to gauge your readiness for the exam, to better understand the objectives being tested, and to get a broad exposure to the DB2 11 knowledge you'll be tested on. The book is also a fine introduction to DB2 for z/OS!

DB2 Exam C2090-313 Practice Questions

ISBN 13: 978-1534992467

This book will help you pass IBM Exam C2090-313 and become an IBM Certified Application Developer - DB2 11 for z/OS. The 180 questions and answers in the book (three full practice exams) offer you a significant advantage by helping you to gauge your readiness for the exam, to better understand the objectives being tested, and to get a broad exposure to the DB2 11 knowledge you'll be tested on.

DB2 Exam C2090-615 Practice Questions

ISBN 13: 978-1535028349

This book will help you pass IBM Exam C2090-615 and become an IBM Certified Database Associate (DB2 10.5 for Linux, Unix and Windows). The questions and answers in the book offer you a significant advantage by helping you to gauge your readiness for the exam, to better understand the objectives being tested, and to get a broad exposure to the knowledge you'll be tested on.

About the Author

Robert Wingate is a computer services professional with over 30 years of IBM mainframe programming experience. He holds several IBM certifications, including IBM Certified Application Developer – DB2 11 for z/OS, and IBM Certified Database Administrator for LUW.   His experience includes creating and supporting systems hosted by DB2, MS SQL Server, Teradata, Informix and PostgreSQL. He lives in Fort Worth, Texas.